THE
SINGLE
MOM'S
GUIDE
to FINDING JOY
in the CHAOS

ELSA KOK COLOPY

Revell

Grand Rapids, Michigan

© 2006 by Elsa Kok Colopy

Published by Fleming H. Revell
a division of Baker Publishing Group
P.O. Box 6287, Grand Rapids, MI 49516-6287
www.revellbooks.com

Printed in the United States of America

Library of Congress Cataloging-in-Publication Data
Colopy, Elsa Kok.
   The single mom's guide to finding joy in the chaos / Elsa Kok Colopy.
      p.   cm.
   Includes bibliographical references.
   ISBN 10: 0-8007-3066-6 (pbk.)
   ISBN 978-0-8007-3066-6 (pbk.)
   1. Single mothers—Religious life. 2. Mother and child—Religious aspects—Christianity. 3. Child rearing—Religious aspects—Christianity. 4. Parenting—Religious aspects—Christianity. I. Title.
   BV4529.18.C65   2006
   248.8'431—dc22   2005036758

Published in association with the literary agency of Alive Communications, Inc., 7680 Goddard Street, Suite 200, Colorado Springs, CO 80920.

To my teenager who was once
a preschooler—Sam Kelly Lynch.
Life with you is a sweet adventure.

And to my husband, Brian Colopy,
who has added (in wonderful ways)
to the joyful chaos of our world.

Contents

Contents

Part 4: Let's Get Practical

Part 5: Your Spiritual Well-Being

Introduction

I can almost picture you. You have a touch of peanut butter in your hair, a smudge of grease on your cheek, and more than one broken fingernail. You're tired and probably hungry. And the last time you did something for yourself was when you bought this book—eight months ago.

I understand! I was a single mother for twelve years. My daughter is thirteen years old, and I'm just now getting the peanut butter out of my hair. It's been an incredible run, and I know that I still have some of the best years ahead of me.

I can tell you this: my daughter did survive the preschool years. She not only survived, she seemed to laugh pretty regularly, to create with abandon, and to learn most of the English language. As a mom, I sometimes did things well. Sometimes I fell flat on my face. I read to her every night but had no patience when she was hyper. I loved to play with her but on many days simply didn't have the energy. I made good decisions and bad ones. I climbed in and out of debt and worked all types of hours, from full-time plus to part-time. I did day care, pre-preschool, and preschool. And I learned.

This book deals with many of the things I encountered as a single parent of a preschooler. I talk about play, learning, discipline, and imagination. For you, I share tips on relationships, budgeting, friendships, and dreaming big. Within each chapter you'll find help with parenting your preschooler and tips for keeping your own sanity. At the end of each chapter you will discover some extra resources that deal specifically with that topic—just in case you find some more time to read.

But first, before you even begin, I have something to tell you. You are amazing! You have one of the hardest jobs on the face of the earth. You're in charge of finances, discipline, love, laughter, household chores, dishes, laundry, dinners, kitchen floors, bedrooms . . . the list goes on. I get tired just writing about it! You have to keep your cool, you have to be responsible, you have to be "Mom." You are a *hero*! And you have my utmost respect.

My guess is that you may not feel the same way. You're probably pretty hard on yourself. Instead of thinking about the thousand things you get done, you focus on the few that you missed. So hear me on this—this book is not allowed to induce guilt. It's meant to be an encouragement. Every chapter deals with a different subject, but that does not mean you have to incorporate all twenty chapters into your daily life over the next six weeks. These are points to think about. Read the chapter, and if it applies to one of your dire needs, address it. If it deals with something that you are already doing, or that you don't need help with, then move on with a smile. But whatever you do, don't allow it to be another piece of baggage to add to your load.

I want to encourage you to consider reading this book with a friend. There are so many things to think about, you may find it helpful to bounce ideas off another single mom. In fact, you can get together and let the kids play while you have some time to yourselves. This alone will do you a world of good.

I want you to know that I will be praying for you. I will pray for strength, for encouragement, for hope. I will pray that you will find what you need within these pages and that you will feel equipped to carry out your role as a single mom. Your life is a testimony to so much good. You are a survivor, a fighter, the woman in charge. I wonder if you see the beauty, resilience, and strength that come from this season of life. I pray that you will, even as you continue through these pages—for you *are* beautiful, friend—peanut-butter clumps, greasy smudges, and all.

Warmly,
Elsa

Part 1

Relationships 101

1

Friendship

It was hard for me to control my laughter. Sami was straddling the ottoman, her little feet dangling off the edge. "I'm gonna catch you!"

Her friend Amanda squealed and pretended to gallop away. "You are not!" she yelled as she crawled quickly and hid behind the curtain.

Sami jumped off her pretend horse and, with all her four-year-old might, she pushed it a few inches. Then she jumped back on. "I'm coming fast now!"

She jumped off again and pushed it another few inches. Amanda squealed louder. "You can't catch me—I'm a superhorse!"

"Oh yeah?" Sami said, going through her whole routine again. "Look how fast I'm coming!"

Amanda crawled out from behind the corner and giggled. "You're not coming very fast at all; I think your horse is a slowpoke!"

Sami climbed off and looked at the ottoman. She pushed it; it only moved a few inches. "You're right," she said. "I'll just chase you myself!"

With that the girls ran up the stairs, squealing and giggling louder than ever.

I couldn't help but laugh as I watched them. Two beautiful girls totally consumed in chasing each other with an ottoman. I mean, when was the last time I'd straddled a piece of furniture and giggled my way through the afternoon? And I loved hearing Sami laugh. It did my heart good to know she was enjoying a friend on a Saturday afternoon. It made our family feel normal in a way I couldn't really define.

Later that night, Sami curled up beside me during our bedtime snuggle. "I had so much fun today, Mommy. Amanda is my best friend in the whole world. Thanks for letting her come over."

Moments later, as I sneaked out of the room and shut off the light, Sami was sleeping soundly, a smile on her face. This had been a good day.

Friendships Matter

Sometimes getting our kids connected to their friends takes a lot of effort. Here are some thoughts to help inspire you on the way.

Friendships foster laughter. Sami and I always put a high priority on laughter, but sometimes the tasks of life take over and life gets altogether too serious. Saturday chores replace Saturday tickles. "Getting things done" becomes the highlight of the day. Because much of our time is structured, playtime with friends (with no particular agenda) doesn't come around as often as I like. But when it does, when we make it a point to invite a child over (even now that Sami's a teenager), their giggles seem to light up the house in a way housecleaning never does. Think about it, single-parent homes can easily fall into the too-serious category—and not without good reason. There's much to do and only one adult to take care of it all. But kids *do* need to be kids. It does them so much good to think about nothing more than how to make an inanimate object animate, to create a story out of pebble figures, or to giggle loudly and with abandon.

Friendships help kids develop social skills. It's important for kids to interact with kids. They learn all kinds of social skills from a morning of play. They learn how to share, to imagine, to give, to laugh, to compromise. They learn what it means to fight and make up, to take turns, to talk, and to listen. We can talk about sharing all day long, but when a child is facing a good friend and that friend is pleading for the toy in your child's hands, suddenly the lectures take on new meaning. They have to learn what it does to a relationship to share and what it does when they hoard. As they experience some of those natural consequences, they will grow socially and relationally. Our kids need friends to help teach them how to interact with their world.

Friendships expand a child's world. One of Sami's best friends was a girl named Amber. Amber and Sami hit it off big. Amber came from a bigger family—she had a little brother, two sisters, and a sweet mom and dad. Not only that, Amber's mother loved animals. They had cats, dogs, birds, even a snake or two. Sami loved to spend time there because not only did she love the big family chaos, she loved the animals, the games, the wrestling, the tickling, and the teasing. There was always something happening at Amber's house, and for Sami, it was very different from the quiet life she knew with me. Her friendship with Amber expanded her world.

Friendships give you a break. I'd had a stressful week, so when Sami asked to have a friend over, I was hesitant. It just felt like more work—even to go pick up the girl from her home. Finally, I agreed. With sighs meant to remind my girl how big this favor was, off we went. We came back home, and I sent the girls to Sami's room to play with all her stuffed animals. I started working on the kitchen, piddling around, cleaning up and organizing drawers. I was totally surprised when Sami and her friend came downstairs two hours later. I had no idea that much time had passed. Not only does friendship offer play for your children, develop their social skills, and expand their world, it also gives you a break—and that's a good thing.

So now you know friendships matter, but you're not sure where to start. Here are two ideas that may help smooth the process as you help your kids build and enjoy friendships.

Develop opportunities. Keep an eye out for kids your child may connect with either at church, at your MOPS group, or at preschool. Your child will probably have no trouble voicing a few favorites. From there, hang around at the end of school or class and introduce yourself to the parent. Ask about a playdate. Something as simple as going to a park or a nearby playground would work great.

Trade off with another single parent. There are other single moms of preschoolers around, and I guarantee they could use a break as much as you. How wonderful it would be if you could trade off on alternate Saturdays.

Even if you tried for once a month, think how nice it would be for you to have a Saturday free and for your child to have a regular playdate with a new friend. Keep your eyes open and make the request. It will be worth it for both of you.

Your Turn

I used to consider myself a lone rangerette. Sure, I had friends, but most of them were more like acquaintances. I didn't spend a lot of time on the phone; I didn't need to go to other people with my problems. I was a rock—or so I told myself. In fact, I was more interested in developing friendships with guys than with women. At least those scenarios were more fun. There was more potential for flirting and affirmation. I didn't see what the big deal was about girlfriends—what could they really offer me? And weren't most women pretty catty? Why would I need that in my life?

Yikes! I look back, and I'm amazed. Now I can't imagine what I'd do without my girlfriends; they make me laugh, they let me vent, they remind me that I'm beautiful when I'm having a horrible hair, body, and clothing day. They are my lifelines to God's heart. I don't want to be a rock. I don't want to do life alone. I'd much rather call Jennifer, Gretchen, Jan, or Carol. They know just what to say to make me laugh.

Why the shift? I think it started when the guy thing let me down on a continual basis. It continued as I realized I wasn't so different from other women—most of us have the same longings to love and be loved, to know and be known. It grew as I understood that women, in general, have a desire and a gift to nurture each other and will stand by you when the boys have long since run for the hills. I came to treasure the women in my life when I learned I could be completely me and they would still love me. I came to treasure them when I realized how pitifully I did life on my own, how being a rock made me hard and stiff and boring to be around, and how being the lone rangerette wasn't as cool or noble as I thought it would be.

Why Friendships Matter

Friendships help us battle loneliness (and the choices that come with that). When I isolated myself, I found it much easier to make lousy choices in relation to men or chocolate cake. I could easily overindulge in either because I was looking for a quick fix to the loneliness that seemed to consume me. But as I developed some real friendships with good women, they became my safe place. Rather than chocolate cake, I could call Jennifer. Rather than succumbing to temptation and calling a guy I knew wasn't good for me, I could hang out with Gretchen and Carol. They eased my loneliness in very real and significant ways.

Friends help us laugh. I love Gretchen. She's a very cool, brilliant, creative, wild woman. She's a gifted musician and also a nurse practitioner. She's a beautiful combination of detailed intelligence and out-of-the-box creativity. And Gretchen makes me laugh. One Christmas she started a tradition in our family by bringing over a mystery gift. It was a lone branch buried in a pot. Hanging from its barren limb was the casing from a bullet. "It's a riddle," she told us, her demeanor very serious. "You'll have to figure it out."

Well, we stared at that bullet. We stared at the branch. We looked at each other and shrugged our shoulders. Not one of us had a single clue.

Later that day, she sang the traditional carol for us: "Five golden rings, four calling birds, three French hens, two turtledoves, and a cartridge in a bare treeeeeee."

The following Christmas, she presented two purple gloves (two turtledoves), and the year after brought three fish heads (three French hens). Gretchen took the normal, everyday things of life and made them funny. I desperately needed her in the midst of the heartache and struggle and seriousness of single parenthood.

A friend is someone we can gripe to (instead of our kids). "I hate everyone and everything!" I said as I flopped down on Jennifer's couch. "And I mean it. Everyone and everything!" She just laughed at me. And we talked. We talked about the jerk who had cut me off in traffic; we talked about my tight pants and the horrible new store-bought color of my hair. We talked about work and finances and how I was sick and tired of having absolutely no money to my name. And somehow, at the end of our conversation, I felt better. Nothing changed, and after bagels and cream cheese, my pants were even tighter. But life was looking up—because Jennifer listened.

Girls, we need someone we can be real with—someone we can feel safe to bare our souls to, someone who knows our heart and lets us gripe so we can see the situation for ourselves. If we don't get our feelings out, they will come out in unhealthy ways. We'll gripe at our kids or grump at our boss or beat ourselves up. But if we have a safe place to go with our hurts, we can face life again, usually with a smile on our face.

A friend is someone we can encourage. I can't tell you how good it felt to be needed. Jennifer called me on one of *her* bad days, and I was able to listen and encourage her. At the end of the phone call, she was so grateful. I hadn't done much, but it made a difference to her. What an incredible thing! After having made some poor choices in my life and in my world, it felt so good to do something beneficial for someone else. And as I began to build other friendships, as I began to grow in that area of my life, that became a huge blessing. I was thrilled I had something to offer someone else, that I could make someone's day brighter. We not only need safe places to go, we need to be a safe place for others. It's an amazing thing when someone entrusts us with the hurt in his or her story.

How to Make Friends

Maybe making friends doesn't come easily to you. That's okay. Here are some tips that may help you.

Talk to people from different walks of life. The Jennifer I've been talking about is a married mom of five. One of my other dear friends is a married mother of three. I have friends who are single women, friends who are single parents of little ones, and friends with grown kids. I have friends who are twice my age and some who are way younger. Don't limit yourself to a certain type of person. Each individual has a story, with all the accompanying heartbreak, adventure, and joy. Whether young or old, married or single, each one can offer something different to your world. Don't limit yourself; if you connect with someone, reach out and go for it. Don't let differing life circumstances deter you.

Don't be afraid to initiate. I used to think people should reach out to me. After all, I was a single mom, and I needed people to take the first step. I was easily offended when people didn't pay as much attention to me as I thought they should. Didn't they see? Oh, I didn't think it through that specifically, but my irritation showed up in my actions. I'd been through rough circumstances; why didn't anyone reach out to me? Honestly, most people didn't know I wanted them to reach out, and if they did know, they usually didn't have the time. I'm not sure when it started, but I decided to reach out instead of waiting for others to do the same. I brought coffee and bagels to Jennifer on Thursday mornings; I invited another woman to work out with me and another to church. I gave up tallying who called whom and pouting when I didn't receive my quota of calls. I wanted friendship. It was worth the investment. And the payoff has been amazing.

Get together with kids. The cool thing about getting together with other moms is you can include the kids. Sami has grown up with Jennifer's kids. When I went to Jennifer's house, I brought Sami with me. Playdates are a great opportunity for moms and kids to develop friendships. Two birds with one stone!

Schedule time for friends. I don't live near Jennifer anymore. I'm in Arkansas; she's in Missouri. But we still talk, every Thursday morning at 6:30. We're committed to that. When we lived near each other, we met every other Saturday morning for coffee. If you can commit to a regular time (a lunch, playdate, phone conversation), you will make it happen. Without being strategic, your time will go by the wayside. Life is busy enough, so it's important to schedule the time for friends.

Bottom line: Friendship is one of the key ingredients that will help you in this season of life. Friends are important for you and important for your children. They'll be the sunshine when everything else seems dismal. And honestly, girls, there are times when we could all use a healthy dose of sunshine. Go for it.

Additional Resources

Brestin, Dee. *The Friendships of Women*.

_____. *The Joy of Women's Friendships*.

Elkins, Stephen. *Friendship and Kindness: The Greatest Bible Stories Ever Told*, Vol. 8.

Graham, Vicky, compiler. *A Breath of Kindness: Expressions of Friendship*.

Mullins, Traci. *Celebrating Friendship* (Women of Faith Series).

2

Sibling Rivalry

● ●

John didn't like me—and I think I know why. John is the youngest of my four older brothers, and when I was born, I had the audacity to take his place as the youngest. Then, to add insult to injury, I had to go and be a girl. And finally, the kicker of all? I had dimples.

Everyone made a big deal about me, my dimples, and my girlness. And John lost some of the spotlight.

It wasn't pretty. From the moment I could crawl, John took great delight in pushing me over, grabbing my hair, and stealing my toys. We fought before I knew how to talk, and things only escalated once words came in.

We drove my mom crazy, and she tried everything to get us to get along. She talked to us, punished us, separated us, and forced us to spend time together.

Now, thirty years later, John has five kids of his own. Two of his middle children have the same love-hate relationship. John tells them stories of what he used to do to me and the punishment he endured. He even tries to tell them how it's much better to avoid the heartache and just love each other. The kids won't hear of it. They still push, shove, yell, and pull hair.

It's unavoidable. Brothers and sisters will fight. Your children aren't any different than kids growing up in other homes. So let's look at what you can do, for even in the midst of the fray there is hope.

What You Can Do

Why is it that kids fight? Why can't they "all just get along"? If you have more than one child, you understand sibling rivalry. It happens.

First, know that you're not alone. My friend Andrea is the single mother of five children. I thought it was a big job raising my one girl; she's raising five kids. One of the biggest hurdles for her is dealing with the frequent wrestling matches, screaming, pinching, and teasing. But she has a handle on it. Her kids fight, but she's come up with some creative ways to distract them. And most days she seems mostly sane. I asked Andrea what she does to help the situation, and she gave me some pointers to pass along.

Talk family. From the beginning, Andrea talked family. She reminds the children they should never take for granted the gift they have in each other. She tells the older kids to look out for the younger and the younger to respect the older. Sure, sometimes she feels like she's a broken record and no one's hearing the tune, but she keeps at it. She shared with me how on one occasion, her oldest son, James, stepped up for his siblings.

"He was herding the younger kids through the church office. We were there so I could speak with one of the pastors, and I asked James to keep an eye on the younger kids. He got them settled in one of the rooms and then asked a secretary to watch them just while he went to the restroom. On the way back, one of the church staff who knew him stopped him as he walked by. 'James,' he said, 'would you like a lollipop?'

"'Yes, please,' he said, then stopped. 'But I can't have one unless I can bring one back for my brothers and sisters.'

"The staffer looked through his candy jar and found he only had three other lollipops. 'You're welcome to have them all, James, but it's not quite enough.'

"'That's okay; I'll just give them to the others.'

"When I heard about his reaction, I about fell over. Somewhere along the line, he'd heard my constant chatter about looking out for his younger siblings. Now granted, stuff like that doesn't happen often—he's just as likely to swipe a lollipop as give it away—but on this one day, this one moment, he got it. And it gave me hope."

If your kids are at each other constantly, be at them constantly with the concept of family. Remind them of how much they should matter to each other. Encourage them to stand up for each other; let them know how many kids wish they had brothers and sisters and how wonderful it is to have family. While they may not get it at the moment, the message will ultimately ring in their own minds as well.

Be firm. "I just can't tolerate the pushing, shoving, or pinching," Andrea says. "It's hard enough to get some food on the table, get them to do their homework, and get the younger ones bathed and in bed. They *have* to get along if the evening is ever to end with my sanity intact."

Andrea has strict rules about her kids getting physical with each other. If they choose to hit, punch, or shove, they are in immediate time-out, they lose privileges, or they go to bed early. It doesn't matter who started it, why it happened, or how offended either of the parties appears to be. "I just can't do it—and because they know that I'm unwavering in that, they tend to keep physical harm to a minimum."

Whenever my mom reprimanded my brother and me, we knew she meant business. Both John and I shut our mouths. No questions asked. If your kids know that your threats are real, they'll obey. On the other hand, if they know that sometimes you let it slide, or sometimes you don't follow through, they'll risk it—hoping this will be one of those times.

Don't be afraid to set ground rules (and stick by them) for sibling interaction.

Offer distractions. While you don't want kids pushing, hitting, or shoving, give them other opportunities to get physical. Gather them together for some family basketball, football, or wrestling. Let the little ones release their energy in other healthy ways. A child is never too young to learn how to play kickball, to throw around a Nerf football, or to get outside and run. My mom used to make us run around the house three times. Of course, at the time, we thought it was all in fun, just to race each other. Now, looking back, I figure she just wanted us to get out the energy that was driving her insane. But we did it, and we were usually laughing by the end.

That woman knew what she was doing.

Remove yourself. "I used to try to hear out every argument, weigh the sides, and try to come up with the fairest outcome," Andrea says. "But I gave up on that. I ended up spending all my time talking through petty fights about who didn't flush the toilet and who stole whose underwear. I was done! So I decided to create a 'conflict corner.' I know," she laughs. "It sounds cheesy, but it actually worked. They'd be fighting, and I'd send them downstairs to the 'conflict corner' (as far out of earshot as possible). They had to stay there as long as it took to figure it out. Once they did figure it out, they could come upstairs and tell me their solution. I didn't give them the chance to raise another argument, I just wanted to hear the result of their conversation. It pretty much took the steam out of half their fights because they usually started them to get my attention anyway. Then, when they came up with their solution, I'd scoop them up, give them kisses, and congratulate them for working it out on their own. It saved me a ton of grief. I wish I'd thought of it sooner!"

Maybe you don't have a big enough house to send kids out of earshot. That's okay; send them wherever you have to and encourage them to work through their own issues. Before you do that though, you may want to explain compromise and forgiveness. Show them ways to work through conflict by role-playing with them. Even the youngest kids will get a kick out of acting out an argument and working it through with you. Help them to see and understand that not every argument has to end with somebody's head under someone else's armpit.

Are there going to be times this won't work? Yes, when someone gets physical (go to plan A for time-out or loss of privileges), or if you know exactly who the culprit is and you can address it swiftly. And of course, if your children are too young (i.e., the two-year-old is fighting the four-year-old), this won't work. But otherwise, give them the opportunity to work through stuff on their own. Not only will it save you some grief, it will equip kids to work through conflict when they're older.

Know thyself. One of the frustrating things about kids fighting is how quickly our blood pressure can shoot through the roof. "I have to be so careful," Andrea says. "I can't hand things off to my husband when I've reached my limit. When I'm at the end of my rope, there's only me. That can be a dangerous situation. I can lose my temper and say things totally out of line with the offense. There have been times when I've had a bad day at work, come home to fighting, and lost my cool in the most embarrassing ways. But after a few times, I learned. When I'm at the end of myself, I need to take a break. I give myself a time-out before I deal with it. So I go into the other room, say a prayer, and ask God to keep me calm. It helps. Otherwise there are just moments when I can't see straight—and the kids get the brunt of a whole day's worth of frustration."

Model forgiveness. "One of the best gifts I learned to give my kids was forgiveness," Andrea shares. "There are times when they cross a line and say something totally inappropriate to me or to their siblings. The younger ones will sometimes have a harder time controlling tantrums. They won't necessarily say anything out of line, but they'll have a hard time controlling their bodies when they're angry. So they might hit or throw themselves on the floor or get totally dramatic. I found that when we talk it through and they ask for forgiveness, I have an opportunity to show them what forgiveness looks like. I can either accept their apology and hold them close—or I can teach them what unforgiveness looks like by snapping at them or refusing (with my actions) their apology."

Modeling forgiveness is one of the benefits of helping children through sibling rivalry. Both asking for forgiveness and extending it are important concepts to learn. The multitude of sibling arguments gives ample opportunities to learn both.

Be optimistic. Hold on to the fact that the relationships your kids share with each other really do matter to them, even if it doesn't seem like it now. My brother John tells the story of a trip my mom and I took when I was eight years old. He went with my dad to drop us off at the airport. We fought the whole way there. But on the way back, once I was gone, he was miserable. "I missed you so much," John says now. "I never would have admitted it to you then, but I couldn't stand being without you. Despite everything, you were still my little sister—and probably my closest friend."

And that's what you have to remember. Even on the worst days, cling to the fact your kids do love each other; it's just in this season that love plays out in various tortures and teasing. And remember too—all this will come to an end. Kids do grow up; they eventually move out of the house and on their own. And hopefully, as you've promoted family and given them the tools to work through arguments, they'll go out better able to face the world because of their interaction with their siblings.

Bottom line: Don't let sibling rivalry destroy the peace in your home. Be firm, don't tolerate violence, and let your children work through issues on their own. If you need to, take a break from the chaos. Hide out in the garage or sneak into the bathroom for an extended moment alone. Then take several deep breaths and remember: this too shall pass.

Additional Resources

Cartmell, Todd. *Keep the Siblings, Lose the Rivalry: 10 Steps to Turn Your Kids into Teammates.*

Dobson, James. *The New Strong-Willed Child.*

Faber, Adele, and Elaine Mazlish. *Siblings Without Rivalry: How to Help Your Children Live Together So You Can Live Too.*

Sande, Ken, with Tom Raabe. *Peacemaking for Families: A Biblical Guide to Managing Conflict in Your Home.*

3

Sacrifices

Sami called, her enthusiasm splashing through the phone and washing over me. "Mom! It's so cool! Daddy has a huuuuge pool! He has floaties and tiki lights and a big grill—and, Mom, he cooked me hot dogs and everything! We played all afternoon, and Dad threw me all over the place in the water. It was so fun!"

"That's great!" I said, trying my best to mean it. "I'm happy for you!"

"Okay, Mom, I have to go now. I love you!"

"I love you too . . ."

The phone went dead. I looked outside at our own big and happenin' pool. It was round, six inches deep, and at this point in the summer, full of green slime and various critters. I didn't even fit in the thing, much less fit with Sami so I could throw her "all over the place." Our grill? A tiny thing on two legs propped up on the other side by a pile of rocks. And tiki lights? How about a flashlight leaning against a tree stump?

I sighed. It didn't seem fair, and sometimes it was hard to celebrate with Sami when she experienced so much fun—away from me. Of course I wanted her to have a good relationship with her dad, but I hated feeling as if everything in our home paled in comparison to the things she got to do and see with him.

I shook my head. It didn't matter. I had to be bigger than all that. What mattered was she had a relationship with her father. She needed him in her world. It was up to me to suck it up and do what I could to help make the relationship strong and encourage it when I could. Wonderful.

Dads Matter

Can you relate? Some of you do. Others don't. It could be that you're a widow and you wish your husband were around to be part of your child's life. Or maybe your child's father has disappeared from both of your lives, or is a danger to you or your child. If that's your story, keep reading. There is some help for you in this chapter as well. But if you do struggle with some of the feelings I shared, then you understand it can be hard to hear about the wonderful weekend your ex and the kids spent together, about the cool new game Dad bought, or the three times they went out to eat in two days. So let's look at the value of the father-child relationship. It matters, and sometimes we need to remind ourselves why.

A good father-child relationship builds joy. Little boys and girls need both their parents—and having a quality relationship with both only enhances their world. If you've been through a divorce, it's important to remember that your child didn't divorce the other parent. As much as the two of you don't get along, in your child's eyes, neither of you could do wrong. They long for connection to both Mom and Dad, and getting that time will add tremendous joy to their lives.

A good father-child relationship builds security. If you have been through a divorce, nurturing your children's relationship with their father will build much needed security. Children need to know that even though their world has changed and Mom and Dad no longer live together, they will always have the security of being welcomed and enjoyed in both homes.

A good father-child relationship builds confidence. When a child feels unloved or somehow abandoned by one or the other parent, it strips them of their confidence. They won't believe or even be able to understand that the lack of relationship has nothing to do with them—instead they will own it. They'll think there is something wrong with them and that's why the other parent doesn't love them or want to spend time with them. By encouraging the relationship between your child and his or her dad, you give the child the gift of confidence, knowing that he or she is loved and valued by both parents.

How to Encourage a Good Father-Child Relationship

If you can, encourage the relationship your children have with their father. It builds joy, security, and confidence. If and when you have the opportunity to do so, here are some tools that may help.

Help father and child spend time together. I'd just gotten a reliable set of wheels, and we headed out for a road trip. Sami, at seven years old, had no idea where we were going, and I wasn't about to tell her. It was a summer afternoon, I had five days off, and we were on the road. I told her it was a surprise but that she'd love it when we got there. Her dad lived far away, almost a thousand miles, so she didn't get to see him very often. I decided to take her there myself. I called her dad and set it up. The next night Sami and I arrived in Virginia Beach and sat in our small hotel room. She still had no idea where we were; she hadn't made the connection between the beach signs and the fact that her dad lived near a beach.

We made a little game of it, and I made her guess who might live near the ocean. She guessed several other friends before she looked at me, her eyes lighting up, her smile growing brighter. "Is it Daddy? Am I going to get to see my daddy?"

I nodded my head and she went nuts. She grabbed me around my neck, held me close, and squealed. "My daddy! My daddy! Thank you! Thank you, Mom!!!"

Tears immediately sprang to my eyes. I hadn't done many things well with her through the divorce, but I knew this was the best decision I'd made in a long time. The next morning, her dad came to get her and they spent three days together. They played in the pool, enjoyed the tiki lights, and she ate hot dogs to her heart's content.

When I saw her smile as she hugged her dad close, I couldn't begrudge either of them a minute of that time. She loved her dad. She needed him. And he needed her.

Some things are worth the sacrifice. Whether it's letting your children see their dad on holidays or during the summer, or whether it's on alternate weeks, do what you can to allow your child time with the other parent. It makes a difference.

Keep from speaking poorly about your child's father. My friend Daniel grew up hearing horrible things about his dad. His mom was so bitter from the divorce, she wanted to make sure her ex never had a relationship with their son and their son would never want to reach out to him. "But it ended up having the opposite effect," Daniel says now. "For a long time I hated my dad, thinking he'd abandoned us. Later, I learned from a friend of the family that he'd tried to stay in contact but my mom kept us from him. Now, I've reconnected. He's not a perfect man, but he's a good man. We're friends. But," he went on, "I have a hard time with my mom. I'm angry that she kept me from him and that she always talked about him. I could have had a dad all this time; why couldn't she let me love him?"

What Daniel experienced isn't uncommon. Unfortunately, many divorced parents have a hard time speaking kindly and encouraging their child's relationship with the other parent. But it matters, not only for the child to have a relationship but also to help the child feel good about their own identity. Remember, your child is a combination of both parents. When you put the other parent down, you put the child down. You encourage a good relationship when you refuse to say unkind things about the other parent.

What If Dad's Not Around?

If you're a widow, or if your child's father hasn't been a part of his or her life since the beginning, or if it isn't safe for your children to spend time with their father, that doesn't mean you can't provide a positive male figure for them. Many churches have a mentoring program where individuals in the men's ministry will take boys from single-parent homes out for a hike or camping. Boy Scouts of America offers opportunities for boys to get connected with honorable men. Girls may do well with their grandfather or uncle. Find godly influences and invite them to be a part of your family.

When I was all broken and Sami was just a preschooler, I spent a lot of time at my brother's house. My brother was kind to Sami and being with him gave her an opportunity to relate to an older man. Our kids may not have a dad in their world, but it should be a priority for us to find positive male influences. Some folks (okay, occasionally I've thought this way) think it's a good idea to use this as an excuse to date. Because Sami's dad lived far away, I thought it would be good to remarry and give her a positive male influence. But the problem was I wasn't healthy enough to be dating, much less to consider remarriage. And I knew at the core I wasn't being noble on Sami's behalf; my dating was actually all about me. So I would encourage you not to date and instead seek out emotionally healthy people for your children to spend time with. It will make a difference.

Your Turn

Remember the story I shared in the beginning? About my ex-husband's big pool and my own comparisons? I hated that I didn't have the same stuff to offer Sami, and I was frustrated that I was living hand-to-mouth while he was cooking up hot dogs and steaks and lighting tiki lights. Envy. And it wasn't pretty.

But honestly, envy really hurts only us. We have to set it to the side or it will rob us of life. We truly cannot begrudge our children the joy and relationship they have with their dad. As we love our children, as we long for them to know future success, we should celebrate the relationship they have with their dad. The more love they have, the more chances they have to play and embrace and live life, the better off they will be. We are best served and our kids are best served if we encourage and celebrate those good times with them. It's like when parents have more than one child. The first child is always concerned that Mom and Dad won't have enough love to go around. But our hearts expand. The more we love, the more love we have to give. By encouraging the relationship our kids have with their dad (and maybe a stepfamily), the more love will spill back on us. Our children won't feel pulled in two different directions; they won't feel disloyal and have to handle that stress. They'll simply be able to love both sets of families, and we will reap the benefits of that unhindered relationship.

So what can you do with some of your own emotions? How can you best facilitate the father-child relationship without letting it eat you up? Here are a few practical tools that might help.

Beat down the voices. Whenever that voice creeps into your thoughts to remind you that you are not good enough, or to point out your green slimy pool or your small home or lack of fun, interrupt it. Don't give those thoughts room to speak. Battle lies with the truth. What is the truth? Your child won't remember whether your pool was green and slimy, but he or she *will* remember that you played anyway. It won't matter if gifts were big; it *will* matter that they were wrapped up in a smile and accompanied by a look that truly spoke love. Cut into condemnation with the truth: your child needs both parents. Beating yourself up does no one any good, and whether your house is big or not, your child primarily needs to know you love him or her. You don't need money or space or tiki lights to communicate that truth.

Focus on your own home. We talk about this more in another chapter, but all we can control is what goes on in our home. For example, I can make sure that Sami always feels safe. I can make sure she has regular bedtimes and knows lots of laughter and love. I can pray with her at night and giggle with her in the morning. And hopefully, when all is said and done, she will know that she has a safe place to go and a mom who loves her. So focus on your home. Create a safe, fun environment. Give your children what they need and know those investments won't be forgotten—even if it feels like it for a time.

Bottom line: If possible, do what you can to facilitate a father-child relationship. If it means working out meeting times or being flexible about visitation, go with it. If it means swallowing up some of your own frustration or envy, do that. Celebrate when your children come home full of news about the latest get-together. They want to share, not to make you feel bad but to include you in their world—because you matter to them. As they share, put on a smile, give them high fives, and laugh out loud. As they feel freed up to love their dad, they'll love you all the more. That's the beauty of how love works.

If Dad isn't around, seek out positive male influences. Give your child opportunities to experience healthy relationships with other men. And remember, our God is a Father to the fatherless. As we call out to him, he will help us parent.

Additional Resources

Boelts, Maribeth. *With My Mom, with My Dad.*

Hart, Archibald. *Helping Children Survive Divorce.*

Owens, Connie. *Divorce Comes to Our House* (a Warner Press book).

Smoke, Jim. *Growing through Divorce.*

4

Co-Parenting

"Mommy, Mommy! We had cake for dinner! Chocolate cake with chocolate chips! How come we never get to have that here?"

Andrea groaned inwardly even as she plastered on a smile for her son. "Well, we do have chocolate cake, James, just not usually for dinner."

"I know, why not?"

Andrea ushered her son to the bathroom and stuck a toothbrush into his hand. "Well," she thought for a moment as she added a dollop of toothpaste, "mostly because I want you to have some veggies and meat for dinner. Chocolate cake, around here anyway, is for special occasions."

"That's boring!" James announced.

Andrea nudged his toothbrush toward his mouth, hoping to end the conversation. But as she did, she couldn't stop the thoughts from rushing through her mind. *Choco-*

42

late cake for dinner? What was he thinking? And this was going to help James adopt good eating habits? He probably fed him Pop-Tarts for breakfast and potato chips for lunch. Why do I always have to be the responsible one? Doesn't he get it? What kind of father feeds his child chocolate cake for dinner?

"Mom?" James was looking at her impatiently, tooth-paste dripping down his chin. "Mom, you're ignoring me."

"I'm sorry, honey." James opened his mouth for inspection, and she nodded. "Good job."

She tucked him into bed a few minutes later. "I love you, James," she said. "And, remember, even if your dad and I do things a little differently, our love for you is the same. Okay?"

"Okay, Mom," James replied, his eyes starting to droop. Andrea tried not to think about the sugar high crash his little body was probably experiencing. "I love you, Mommy."

She kissed him on the forehead and went to the kitchen. She eyed the phone. She should call his dad and have a little talk about cake for dinner, but she didn't have it in her. That conversation would have to wait—if it ever happened at all.

When Dad Lives Differently

When our kids spend time in two different households, it's inevitable that each parent will have different ways of doing things. What's important at Mom's house might not be nearly as important at Dad's. What is allowed under one roof may not be allowed under the other. So how do we handle that? Whether Mom and Dad are apart because of a broken marriage or a broken relationship, and depending on the relationship you share (civil . . . or not), there *are* some tools that might help in your situation. Read on.

When the Relationship Is Good

You may be fortunate enough to have a good relationship with your child's dad. If so, that makes things easier. You'll be able to talk through concerns. Yet even with a good relationship, it will help to have a plan in place of how to approach the topic. Here are a few tips I've gathered from other single parents in your situation.

Don't bring up old relational issues. Keep your relationship in good standing by separating your co-parenting from any other issue. Stay calm and stay focused on the reason you need to talk. Anna, a friend of mine, didn't handle this well. She will tell you now how she pushed her ex-husband away. "I wasn't thinking about the relationship he had with the kids. I called him often about the kids, because at first he was willing to listen. But I wasn't making those calls for them—even though I said I did." She says, "I was just mad at him. I felt abandoned and I didn't want to let it go. So when it came to something with the kids, I'd call him up and let him have it. It was over stupid stuff too, like a stain on a shirt or a missed vitamin. I just wanted him to know that I was alive, alone, and mad. It worked. He saw how angry I was, but instead of coming back to me with flowers and a sweet apology, he withdrew. He withdrew from me and from the kids."

Do what you can to avoid Anna's mistake. Keep the conversation on your co-parenting, and if you sense you're calling for a different agenda, talk to a friend, vent to her, and ask her to hold you accountable.

Be solution-based. When you talk with your child's dad, have a solution already in mind. Include how you will contribute to the resolution so you feel that you are partnering in the idea.

Keep the focus on your child's best interest. Laura was struggling. Her daughters, Amber and Jillian, spent every weekend with their father. He was a good dad; he just had a problem getting them to bed on time. So when the girls returned home on Sunday evening, Amber didn't want to go to bed. Then it would take three days to get her back on schedule—only to have her routine completely upended the following weekend. It was starting to affect Amber's behavior at preschool and her attitude at home.

Laura thought about it for a few days and then gave David, her ex-husband, a call. She knew he had a harder time with schedules in general (and didn't respond so well to criticism in that area), so she didn't want to come across overly harsh. She knew, too, that if she approached it from the perspective of the girl's best interest, he would be more receptive. So she shared how Amber had a tough time going to bed Sunday evenings and a hard time getting up on Monday mornings. Would he be willing to have her in bed by 9:00 p.m.? She would be grateful.

He agreed, and while he didn't follow through every time, the situation did get better. Laura made sure to express her gratitude. She knew if she did, David would be much more willing to hear her requests in the future.

Stay on what matters. This is where wisdom is needed. Before approaching your child's dad with several suggestions for "how-to" and "how-not-to," think about the issues that are important to your child's health and well-being. Don't nitpick on lots of little items so the relationship becomes tense and uncomfortable. Remember, some things are just going to be different. In order to keep your relationship civil and intact, know what issues matter most to you and stick with those. Let the smaller stuff go.

When Parents Can't Get Along

It would be wonderful if every couple who bore a child put everything else aside to parent that child. It would be amazing if differences could be ironed out and the child thought of first. It would also be wonderful if money grew on trees and chocolate was a mandatory food staple. Life just doesn't turn out that easy. So if you are in the unfortunate situation of struggling with your child's other parent, think through these things. They may help.

Set clear boundaries (don't waver to be liked). Let's go back to our opening story. Andrea didn't want to call her ex-husband because of the stressful relationship they shared. She knew what his response would be—something about her needing to lighten up and "the boy" (that's what he called him) being able to have some fun with his father. So Andrea's temptation was to let James have more chocolate cake at home. "I figured if I couldn't beat him, maybe I should join him," Andrea says. "I knew it was silly, but I didn't want to be the only one standing up for good eating habits. And if James's father wasn't going to do it, I wasn't sure I wanted to either. I didn't want James to hate me just because I made him eat vegetables every day. Why should I have to be the bad guy?"

A lot of single parents struggle with this idea. If there are hardly any rules at the other home, it can seem like a good idea to ease up on some of the rules in their own home or even go completely the other way and increase the rules to balance things out. Resist the temptation to go overboard in either direction. Stand firm on the issues you believe matter. Kids need structure, and while living in a home without rules might seem appealing for a little while, ultimately kids shy away from it. They crave structure and understand that structure communicates love.

Learn when to let go and when to hold on. If there's no cooperation between you and your child's father, you'll have to let most parenting issues go. Unless your child is in danger, you may have to overlook the things that drive you crazy. Obviously, it's not easy, and there will be times when you'll worry, but don't let frustration take too much of your energy. Your child needs that emotional energy—even more so if the other environment is unstable.

You can try, periodically, to bring some of your concerns to the table, but if they're demeaned or misunderstood, you may have to hold your tongue and let it go. Think instead of ways in which you can stabilize your own home so that no matter what comes, your home is one where your child is taught, encouraged, and kept safe.

What You Can Do

Here are some factors that will help keep your home life intact when you don't have control over other situations.

Consistency. By offering your children a routine while under your roof, they'll always know what to expect. They take baths at such-and-such time, then have a story, and then go to bed. Most nights, anyway. Also, make sure your meals offer a variety of healthy choices and have them take a few bites of each. It helps to keep discipline consistent as well. If they are required to do things a certain way at your home, stay consistent in following through with them. Granted, I'm the first to tell you that consistency is difficult to maintain in a single-parent home, but do the best you can. That way, when things are unstable or constantly changing at their dad's house, they'll know that at your house, they can count on things to remain the same.

Safety and love. When you talk about rules, talk about safety. When Sami was little, she got into the habit of suddenly breaking away from me when we walked somewhere. She didn't want to hold my hand to cross the street or stay with me in the store; she wanted to find her own way. Finally, when she nearly ran in front of a car, we sat down and had a talk. I explained to her that I loved her very, very much and the reason she had to hold my hand was so she could be safe. For some reason, she didn't run from me anymore. Of course the tears in my eyes, the redness of my cheeks, and the passion in my voice probably stuck. That car scared me.

I've continued that practice, often giving Sami an explanation for my rules (although sometimes I've said "Because I say so" with a look that gives no room for questioning—but that's the "mom card" we get to pull out as needed). For the most part though, let your child know that your rules are all about love, safety, and protection. That way, when they feel you are being unreasonable (i.e., much stricter than Dad), they'll know the motive behind your decisions.

Warmth. Whether your child has just been to school or just spent time with Dad, welcome him or her home. As much as you are able, be warm and inviting, so that no matter what is happening in the other home, your child knows that when he walks in the door at Mom's house, someone is happy to see him.

Long-term hope. "I used to get so mad at my mom," my friend Jenny says. "She was so strict, and as I got older, I used to complain to my friends about her having custody of me. I was hard on her as a kid and mean to her through my teenage years. She was so unreasonable compared to Dad. She didn't let me go to the movies I wanted to—even if I'd already seen them with my father—and she didn't let me listen to music I liked. She was tough! But now," Jenny smiles, "we're so close. I've apologized a hundred times for how I treated her. I know now that it wasn't easy for her to stand firm, but she was doing it because she loved me and wanted to protect me. I'm glad that I lived with her. I mean, I love my dad, and I always will—but he didn't care enough to discipline me. He let me get away with whatever I wanted. I liked that as a kid, but now, looking back, I just don't think he wanted to be bothered."

Bottom line: For many of us, things we resented as children we feel good about now. So even if your little one is complaining about the lack of freedom or the different guidelines at Dad's house, stand firm. Love generously and laugh often, but don't be afraid to stick by the rules you've laid out. Let your home be warm, consistent, and engaging, and you'll create a safe haven for your little one.

If you get along with your child's dad and are able to keep parenting issues a priority, even better. Say a little prayer of thanksgiving and keep nurturing that relationship.

Additional Resources

Brun-Cosme, Nadine. *No, I Want Daddy!*

Cloud, Henry, and John Townsend. *Boundaries*.

Coleman, William. *What Children Need to Know When Parents Get Divorced*.

Reed, Bobbie. *Life after Divorce*.

Sember, Brette McWhorter. *How to Parent with Your Ex*.

Whiteman, Tom. *Your Kids and Divorce: Helping Them Grow Beyond the Hurt*.

Dating

I met Tim when my daughter was four years old. He lived just a few doors down in the same apartment complex and came to my door one evening with a hot apple pie in hand. He was very handsome *and* he could cook. I didn't stand a chance.

Because Tim and I lived so close, it was easy to connect. We'd often chat in the evening, talking about our lives and what had brought us to that particular moment. Usually, Sami was sleeping as we talked.

We grew closer, and soon things turned romantic. Because he lived practically next door there were no natural boundaries to the speed of our relationship. We began to spend more time together and that meant including Sami. I was lonely. He was lonely. Putting us together was like setting fire to dry sticks. We burned quickly and brightly, and Sami was caught up in the fire.

Seven months after we met, Tim proposed and I accepted. Sami was thrilled. She loved Tim, she loved me, and her little heart was wrapped up in the thought of family.

But it wasn't long before I began having doubts. Tim and I had different belief systems, and they seemed to be growing further apart. Living out different values was going to be incredibly difficult, and our eyes were opening to that reality. For another seven months the relationship continued, getting more and more disjointed. Then it ended.

I will never forget telling Sami that Tim would not be in our lives. She burst into tears. "Now he won't be my daddy!" Her words tore at my heart. I had allowed her to connect with him on a daily basis. He had been involved in every aspect of our lives. And they loved each other.

Sami's biological dad lives far away. Through a divorce, she lost him at eighteen months. Now, at a tender age, another loss was introduced to her life.

In so many ways, I wish it wasn't my life or my daughter that I was using as an example. I have seen the effects of those two losses on my girl. Yet perhaps if I can help you to prevent similar pain, then that personal heartache might contain a silver lining.

Protecting Your Preschooler

How do you really take the time to get to know someone without introducing him to your child? How will you know how he is with your child if they never connect? At what point in the relationship should you allow them to meet? Here are some tips that might help you protect your child's heart, even as you take some steps to expose your own.

Avoid the single-mom temptation. I've seen this in myself and in fellow single moms. Because getting a babysitter is such a hassle, we end up spending time with our dates at our apartment or home. We invite our date over (maybe we wait till our child is in bed) and watch movies. We hang out and talk.

This is dangerous because we are more likely to involve him with our child if he's around the house. If date times take place in the living room, it's also more difficult to take it slow—both physically and emotionally. Set a boundary for yourself before you even begin dating. Decide that you will go through the extra effort to get a babysitter, or to go for lunch instead of dinner, whatever it is you need to do to keep him at a safe distance. This will protect both you and your child.

Take it slow. There's never a reason to hurry into a relationship. I used to think there were exceptions to that, but in truth, there are not. Granted, not all of us are susceptible to rushing into a relationship, but some of you reading this know exactly what I'm talking about. A date turns into nightly conversations, which quickly escalate to phone calls throughout the day, emails, and more dates. Pretty soon, interests outside of the relationship take a backseat to spending time with your new love.

With a child's heart at stake, it's incredibly important to take it slowly. Decide, on the front end, that you will only go on a date once a week. This will put a natural boundary on your yearning to love and will also give you the opportunity to process your feelings more objectively. If you see each other too often, it's easy to blind yourself to what might be red flags. Also, staying focused on your family life will be a huge gift to your child. He or she needs your attention.

Does that sound too tough? Think about it though. You need time with your friends, time with your child, time alone. A week passes pretty quickly when you focus on embracing those priorities!

Be cautious if you're in a relationship already. Maybe you're not on the front end. Perhaps you're waist deep in a relationship and you've been spending lots of time together, children and all. If you see a strong future there, make sure you're not making your whole world revolve around this new person. Be cautious with the hearts involved until you're ready to make a lifetime commitment.

If you're waist deep and the relationship is crumbling, take huge steps backward. I remember staying in my relationship longer, even though I knew it wasn't going to work, because my daughter got along so well with my boyfriend. That was the wrong move. I was letting guilt dictate the course of the relationship. I thought I was protecting Sami's heart by putting off the breakup. Instead I should have initiated the break sooner and saved her some of that pain.

Include others. Imagine that you've met a man of character. You've been dating for several months, and you talk on the phone several times a week. He's someone you're interested in getting to know better, and you're getting all kinds of butterflies and warm fuzzies. Before you fall any further, you want to see how he might connect with your preschooler. That's understandable. But it's a catch-22. You want to see how he interacts so you can determine if this is someone you could be serious with. Yet you don't want to introduce your child unless the relationship is serious.

There is a solution. The best way to introduce your child to someone you're dating is in a group environment. Go out with a group of friends and include the children. See how he engages with your child, and see how your child reacts. Keep it light, whether it's a picnic at the park or a movie. Try to avoid situations where it's just the two of you and the children. That immediately sets your children up to feel like it's a family environment.

Refrain from touching. If you're anything like me, you read that heading and want to toss the book. No touching? I'm a very physical person so I always touch as I speak to people I care about. But I've learned that it's hard on Sami. When I was dating Tim, Sami used to come between us when we held hands. She took our hands apart, grabbed my hand, and said, "My mommy!" I know it's difficult not to touch, but especially in the early stages of a relationship, it's important not to hold hands and kiss in front of your children. They tend to make big assumptions when they see you in such close contact with someone else. That, and it's threatening. When they see someone holding you, their first thought is that you are being taken from them. That's why they shove aside, grab hold, and give looks. They don't want anyone taking their mommy! Save your child some of that frustration and try not to touch in their presence.

If your relationship is advancing and you find yourself envisioning a future, slowly allow this man to spend more time with you and your child. I understand that there are no guarantees, but try to be as certain as possible this relationship has a future before you take that step. How long does that take? Every situation is different.

My first inclination is to say, "You know yourself; just be cautious," but that's not necessarily true. Sometimes we blind ourselves to the truth. Ask people you trust if they see a future for the relationship. They probably know if you have a tendency to fall too quickly, or if you romanticize things a little too eloquently. Get as much counsel as you can. Pray about it. Remember, little hearts bond quickly—until they learn one too many times that the bond will break.

Your Turn

It's not only little hearts that are important to protect in a dating relationship. It's important to protect your own as well. Think about these things as you move forward.

Take it slow. Janice met Frank at a church softball tournament. She was widowed with two young children, and he was recently divorced. They started talking that Sunday afternoon and didn't stop for almost three weeks. Friends and family were concerned about the speed of their relationship, but Janice was convinced she had found her soul mate. She told Frank her life story, she introduced him to the children, and they became inseparable.

It came as a tremendous surprise when Frank suddenly stopped calling. Janice had no idea what had gone wrong, but he was quickly gone from their lives. Two weeks later, she found out the truth. He had gone back to his wife, and they were planning to remarry.

Janice's story is not uncommon. Sometimes our longing for love, for help with the children, for a companion, can be so strong that we fall headfirst and we fall fast.

I've been guilty of this myself. Not only do we need to take it slow in order to protect the hearts of our children, we need to take it slow to protect our own hearts. We too must remember that attaching too quickly can leave us heartbroken and wounded.

Get to know a man's character. Anyone can pull off a bit of romance. Any man with his eye on you can figure out what might make your heart go pitter-patter. Oh, friend, just remember a man of character is about a lot more than roses, dinner, and buttered popcorn at the movies. Look closely at this man you are thinking of letting into your life and the lives of your children. And I don't say this glibly. I'm about as sappy as they get. Roses, chocolate, and a nice card, and I'm a goner. Pitiful.

You need to look for certain characteristics when you begin dating a man. The list could go much longer (and if you need some additional help in this area, see the resources listed at the end of this chapter), but this will get you started:

- *Faith*. A man who loves God first will love you and your children well. It helps if he is accountable to a much higher power than you!
- *Self-control*. You want a man who is able to curb his appetite, whether that appetite is for food, for women, for anger, or for substances that aren't healthy. Each one of us has weaknesses, but be cautious of a man who exhibits active addictive behavior.
- *Integrity*. Does the man treat people with integrity? Is he honest? If he lies to his friends or in his business, he will lie to you.

- *Compassion.* A man who has a heart of service for others will be much more likely to serve and equip his family.
- *Emotional health.* Make sure the man you are dating isn't still dealing with a lot of past issues. If he's been through a divorce or walked through widowhood, make sure he's taken the appropriate time to grieve and grow. If he hasn't, you will pay that price.

These are a few traits that will give you a better opportunity to know success in your dating relationships. If you find yourself attracted to men of the "bad boy" variety, take some time to get help. A "bad boy" might be exciting for a time, but he will ultimately be a powerful influence on your children and a detriment to you. Stay away from him and take the time to get emotionally healthy yourself. As you grow through your own issues, you will find the "bad boys" aren't so attractive anymore.

Don't get physical. We talked about not touching in front of the children. It's also important not to get too intimate away from the children. Maybe it's been a long time since you've been in a physical relationship. Maybe you feel mature enough, able enough, ready to connect with someone in that way.

Don't do it. Sex is not just the meeting of two bodies as a way to offer some relief and connection. It's a physical, emotional, and spiritual bond that was designed to be experienced in the safety of a marriage relationship. For women especially, we get connected at a much deeper level when we expose that part of ourselves. Society would say it's just another way to communicate, but we know better. Deep inside, in that place where we rarely even admit things to ourselves, we know that sex is so much more than a physical release. Save yourself for a man worthy of that prize and save yourself for a relationship that will not disappear after you've been intimate.

Not only will you protect your own heart by remaining pure, you will also teach your child that same value.

You don't have to date. In my last twelve years of singleness, I've really thrown some folks into a quandary. They wanted me to date, they wanted me to fall in love, and they're excited for when that will happen.

But I didn't know if it would.

I had never really given it much thought, but about five years ago, I realized that I didn't *have* to date anyone. That may seem silly, but I'd been so boy crazy since the second grade, I'd never really considered singleness as a long-term option. I'd always felt incomplete without a partner, and I'd always assumed that Sami would be better off if I found a godly male to be involved in her life.

The truth is, you don't have to date. You can make the decision to wait until your child is grown; you can even make the decision to be on your own for good. You are more than able to do that well, and your children can know tremendous success even if you never marry, date, or do any of the above.

Bottom line: If you do date, take precautions. Protect your heart; protect your child's heart. First and foremost, take it slow. You're not in a hurry; remind yourself of that. Don't settle for a man who doesn't have quality character traits and keep the physical boundaries intact. You will be so glad you did.

Additional Resources

Cloud, Henry, and John Townsend. *Boundaries in Dating.*

Kok, Elsa. *Settling for Less Than God's Best? A Relationship Checkup for Single Women.*

Warren, Neil Clark. *Date . . . or Soul Mate? How to Know If Someone Is Worth Pursuing in Two Dates or Less.*

Part 2

On the Lighter Side

6

Play

I didn't like riding Sami's bike. It was small, it had train-ing wheels, and the seat was not made for derrieres of the larger variety. But she looked at me with those big green eyes and simply begged me to play bikes with her. That didn't mean sitting on the sidewalk and cheering her on. It didn't mean walking beside her. It meant scrunch-ing up my long legs, balancing precariously on that tiny seat, and peddling around the parking lot. With my knees bobbing up to my nose, I looked like a cross between a flamingo and a frog. That's why I wore a baseball cap. And the moustache. And the big glasses with the nose attached. Maybe no one would recognize me.

Why'd I do it? Because of Sami. Because when I made my circle around the parking lot, only falling once or twice, I peddled up to where she stood. I braked right in front of her and raised my arms in triumph. And she laughed. She has such a great laugh. Her eyes sparkled and she clapped her hands. "Good job, Mommy! Good job!"

I unfolded myself from the bike, scooped her up in my arms, and gave her a big smooch. She giggled. "Your turn now," I'd say.

She settled on that little bike and wobbled around the parking lot. The cool thing was she took her feet off the pedals and brought her knees up to her nose, just to be like me.

Those were good moments.

Those kind of moments, especially after a full day of work, came far and few between. I would love to say that every time Sami asked, I was out there on that bike, peddling around, laughing out loud.

More often I was settled onto the couch, catching my breath, hoping for a few minutes of quiet. She'd pull my arm or tug on my pant leg, and I'd ask her to wait just a little bit longer: "Mommy needs to rest for a minute."

Then the dishes needed to be done and dinner prepared, and before I knew it, bedtime had arrived. One more day without play. Been there? So let's take a look at the value of play. Maybe that will help inspire us to set aside the time when we can.

Play Matters

Play is fun. Sami needed me to play with her. She needed my attention. She needed to know that I delight in her. Many times I said, "Okay, I'll play, but just for a minute." That didn't feel very good to her. When I said that, it came across just as I was feeling in that moment—like play was an obligation.

Yet when I played with Sami, when I allowed myself to let go, to act silly, to crawl around on the floor and be her horsey, I discovered joy. I found my own delight bubbling up because sometimes it *was* fun to get down on all fours and bump into stuff. Or I took her to throw bread to ducks, and it started out as an obligatory *in order for me to be a good mom, I should take my daughter to throw bread to the ducks. That is what good moms do, and I'll even look like a good mom to anyone passing by.* It went from that to a pleasurable experience of "Oooh" and "Aaaah" and "My, isn't that one a little piggy!"

Play isn't only good for our little ones. It's good for us. It takes the stress from the day and lets it ease off our shoulders. It's hard to think about finances when you're neighing and stomping in valiant horse fashion. It's difficult to think about the dirty dishes when your son has just captured you and tied you up to the leg of a chair.

On one occasion I took Sami to the pool. She always loved the water. We were sitting on the steps, and she decided that dunking me would be great fun. "One time," I cautioned. She pushed my head under and I came up spluttering. She laughed. "Again, Mom, again!" I couldn't resist. She dunked me again. And again. And again. Finally, when I looked like close kin to a drowned rat, she stopped. She put little hands on either side of my face and kissed my nose. "I love you, Mommy," she said. "You're fun."

There is nothing like a spontaneous "I love you" in the middle of play. That sense of connection is worth rug burns on our knees, crayon-cramped fingers, and water up our nose.

Play is healthy. Not only is play fun; it's healthy for us and for our children. Laughter relieves stress, lowers blood pressure, and increases the strength of our immune systems. As single parents, we need all those physical benefits.

It is documented medically (over and over) that laughter and play have positive effects on our bodies and our brains. Yet, there is one benefit that is even greater. It connects us to our kids! It gives us a glimpse of their smile and reminds us why and how much we love them. And yes, sometimes we need those reminders.

How to Play

Jennifer is learning to play. She's the mother of five and is just now learning to play. It's not that she doesn't like to or doesn't want to; she just never learned how. As the only girl in a family of seven children, she had to be responsible. She'd grown up without ever learning the art of play. "I want to get on the floor and let loose with my kids," Jennifer told me, "but instead I end up worrying about the mess we're making, or I'll worry about when I'm going to make dinner, or I'll just get frustrated with the noise level and their playfulness and get totally stressed out!"

It's not unusual for us to have to learn to play. Maybe we've always been the quiet one, or the responsible one, or the grown-up. That's okay. Learning to play is a process like any other, and it begins by setting aside the time. Make a date with your child and then try any one of these ideas:

- Play catch (or as close to "catch" as you can)
- Read a book and use crazy voices

- Ride bikes
- Make up a dance to your child's favorite song
- Color in a coloring book (I've actually found this to be very soothing)
- Jump up and down and see who can jump higher (Sami loved this one)
- Use sidewalk chalk and draw in the sunshine
- Fill balloons with water and toss them at a convenient target (older brother perhaps?)
- Walk to the playground and crawl through the tubes
- Wait till nightfall and look at the stars

Don't worry if playing feels awkward. When you haven't played, it may feel awkward to start. You might feel silly or embarrassed or out of control. Perhaps your whole life you've been told that you don't make messes for no reason, you don't laugh too loudly, you don't get your hands dirty, and you definitely don't color outside the lines. Well, now it's time. Go for it. Start easy, but start.

Learn to savor. The more you play, the more you'll enjoy it. Learn to savor moments without concern over who might be watching, how you might look, or what work you're missing. Grab the moment that is right before you. Look at your child's smile, see that mischievous look in her eye, notice how small her hands are or how pretty her eyes are. Those moments are the very essence of a life well lived as a single parent. Sometimes, a moment is all we have to savor our child. Dirty hands, silliness, and loud laughter are the very things that make all the work and frustration worthwhile. Don't miss these beautiful moments.

Remember the purpose. I have four older brothers; I can remember longing for their attention when I was a little girl. I looked up to them. The things they liked, I liked. The things they didn't like, I didn't like. So when they spent time with me, when they liked me, *I* liked me. When they turned me away, when they said I wasn't quite big enough, strong enough, or fast enough, I felt exactly like that: not enough.

Oh, but when I was included! When I was able to play a game of tag, run bases, or play kickball, I loved it. I felt like the queen of the world when I was seen as fun to play with by the people I most admired.

Your children long for that kind of connection with you. It's not even the act of playing that really touches their hearts; it's just that you find them enjoyable to be around. You are choosing to spend time in their presence with no other purpose than to play. You're not loving them because they've made a good choice, performed well, or made their bed. You're loving them and giving them yourself for no apparent reason at all! Except maybe because their laughter brings a smile to your face. What greater gift can you give your child?

Give yourself grace. While there are lots of good reasons to play, I do want you to remember something: some days you will have it in you to play; other days you won't. It's okay that on some occasions all you can do is open your arms and call your children to curl up in your warmth. It's okay if you send them outside to play with the neighborhood child. It's okay to let them watch a movie or color a picture on their own.

Obviously, it's important to play when you can. Making time for playing should be an important part of your week. But don't beat yourself up if you are unable to play every day. That will just give you a bigger case of the grumpies. And who needs that?

Your Turn

We've acknowledged that play is important for children. Most of us don't have any trouble believing that— we need to play with our kids. The thing we have trouble with is scheduling time for adult play. It's easy to make that our last priority. But in reality, if we can find refreshment, encouragement, and fun outside the daily tasks of life, we will better handle frustrations that come our way. We do ourselves and our children a huge favor by scheduling time to do things we like.

This was a problem for me. For the longest time I didn't even know *what* I liked. I was a pleaser early on and basically adopted the likes and dislikes of those who were important to me. Not until I began to grow into my own person did I discover some of my own interests. I found out that I like bowling (especially when they make the pins glow in the dark). I like playing softball or reading a good book. I enjoy sitting outside and looking at the stars, and I like being with friends whether we do something or not. If you struggle with a similar mindset—*I'm not even sure what I like*—then maybe it's time to try some new things. Try bowling one night, tennis another. See if you actually like romantic comedies or if you might enjoy a quiet night in a coffee shop. Expand your world with some new experiences.

In the reality of my world, I don't go out very often. I typically put the daily grind ahead of any opportunity to get out and about. But then a moment comes, and I realize that if I don't talk to an adult this instant, I might go completely insane.

I would not suggest this same approach for you. Don't wait until you're at the very limit of your patience before you take a break. Schedule some time to get out and engage the world. If you're anything like me, there will always be an issue to hold you up. By the time you think of how you will be able to afford it, when you will get a babysitter, and who's going to take care of dinner, you opt out of taking the time you need.

The following ideas might help.

Call a friend. Your single parent friends need time apart as well. This can be a group project. What if you set aside every Thursday night for play? On that night, you could rotate babysitting so each of you is able to see grown-ups outside the work environment. This offers no-cost babysitting and a group solution that meets the needs of your friends as well.

Investigate cheap fun. Call around, cut out coupons, check on the Internet. Many recreational activities have coupons available around the community. Try giving places a call and let them know that you have a group of single parents starving for some recreation. Would they be willing to offer a discount? Many locations will offer something if you ask. You could also hike in a national park, bring a picnic to the river, fish in the neighbor's pond, or read a book at a small café.

Remember, you're worth the time. I know what you may be thinking right now. *I can't do this! I don't have time, and I'd spend the whole evening feeling guilty any-way.* Please hear me on this. It is important. You need to know laughter, play, and relaxation. You are shouldering an incredible amount of responsibility and there are times when you need to have a break. It is an act of love. You'll be able to love your children better because you will come back with that crease removed from between your eyebrows. They'll enjoy that mischievous glint in your eye. And really, this is a tough job. Sometimes, you just need to think of nothing other than how the chapter will end, which way the pins will fall, or how bright the moon is on a particular night.

Bottom line: Play will pay off for you and your child. It's a healthy reminder that life is sweet, laughter is good, and there is more to the day than bills, employers, discipline, and fast food. That can only be a good thing!

Additional Resources

Books

Kennedy, Marge, and Karen White. *Play and Learn: More Than 300 Kid-Pleasing, Skill-Building, Entertaining Activities for Children from Birth to Age 8.*

Long, Jill Murphy. *Permission to Play: Taking Time to Renew Your Smile.*

Michelli, Joseph. *Humor, Play & Laughter: Stress-Proofing Life with Your Kids.*

Press, Judy. *The Little Hands Big Fun Craft Book: Creative Fun for 2- to 6-Year-Olds* (Williamson Little Hands Series).

Websites

www.MOPS.org—for more articles (and encouragement) on reducing stress and learning to relax

http://mommyandme.com—has fun ideas and opportunities for play

7

Celebrations

●　●　●　●　●　●　●　●　●　●　●　●　●　●　●　●　●　●

It wasn't your typical preschool party. We'd recently moved to a small apartment complex and didn't know many people in the area. I definitely didn't know any preschool kids, clowns, or talking animals. So when Sami's birthday came around, I did the best I could with what I had to work with. I invited my upstairs neighbors—a young couple with a baby in tow. I invited the single girls a couple of doors down and my older mentor friend who was in her sixties. I baked up a fancy little cake (from a box) and made some juice with boatloads of sugar and a small packet of flavoring. We were as set as we were going to be.

Oh sure, I would have enjoyed setting up one of those big bouncy machines or including kids wearing fancy clothes, but it just wasn't my world. And thankfully, Sami didn't seem to mind in the least. She was thrilled to know people were coming over for her, she was getting gifts, and best of all, she was turning into a bigger girl by the moment. It didn't matter that she didn't know the neighbors; she was just glad they knew how to sing "Happy Birthday." She didn't notice I hadn't had time to plan intricate crafts she could keep forever; she was grateful I blew up balloons and hung rainbow streamers.

It was a wonderful day.

I have a video of that afternoon; the camera shook as I laughed and giggled. One shot shows Sami pouring water from her new tea set, handing tiny cups to her new friends. She took her job very seriously as she took orders for half-full to all-the-way full. At one moment she looked at the camera and grinned a toothy smile. Happy as could be, she stated, "I love you, Mommy!"

So maybe I was lacking in crafts and basic party planning. But to Sami, it didn't matter a bit because people were there for her. It was a Sami celebration.

Celebrations Matter

I know I'm not telling you anything new when I say that kids love to be celebrated. They're unabashed in their desire for moments that are all about them. They anticipate the gifts, they love songs sung about them—they want everyone to focus on their particular achievements. With none of the reserve we grown-ups practice, they savor the attention and hope for more. So how can we, as single moms, celebrate our kids when there are a hundred other things to do? Do we have to have parties? And if so, do they have to be big? Does it have to cost a lot of money? Does the afternoon have to include clowns and gift bags and games? And can we do this celebration thing without expending the last bit of energy we have for the week? Maybe this will help. Let's break it down into little celebrations, medium-sized ones, and monster bashes. Incorporate what you can into your world and don't worry about the rest.

Savor little moments. "Watch me, Mom! Watch me!" I couldn't. It was the 700 zillionth time I'd watched Sami spin in a circle, and I was getting dizzy. She held up her arm over her head. Spin. Drop the arm. Hold it up again. Stop. Then she caught me glancing at the TV and she called out, "Watch me, Mom!" She wanted me to notice the way her dress seemed to float every time. She begged for me to see how perfectly she spun. She looked for my smile and waited for my clap—which had been incredibly enthusiastic the first 699 zillion times but was waning as we came up on 700.

Now, looking back, I can see why Sami needed me to notice her. It wasn't about the spinning or the dress. She needed me to see *her*, to smile and be glad for her presence in my world. She needed me to celebrate her very existence.

Celebrating our kids begins with the little moments. It's paying attention when they spin; it's noticing when they call out their achievement. It's saying "Way to go!" when we don't really think it's that impressive to put on a shirt or eat a whole hot dog. Will we do it all the time? No, there are times we'll miss it. But being aware, knowing that it matters, will get us going in the right direction. Notice the small accomplishments today. It matters.

Take advantage of medium moments. The first day of preschool, Valentine's Day, Christmas—each one of these days offers an opportunity to celebrate our kids. But, a celebration doesn't mean you have to run out and get helium balloons, buy a cake, or sing loudly and off-key.

It's just a day that gives you an excuse to go for ice cream, make a little card, buy chocolate, or stay up late. I've made hundreds of cards for Sami over the years. I just fold a piece of construction paper, draw a big smiley face, tell her I love her and why. I've drawn stick figure moms and daughters holding hands. Even as a teenager, she gets a kick out of my goofy love notes. I may not be a big spender, but I want my daughter to know how much she brings joy to my world. I want her to know that she is a gift.

We need to pause. As I read over this last paragraph, I imagine elevator music and angels singing choruses about love and joy. So let me clarify: yes, I've made Sami cards. I've bought chocolate and set it beside her bed for Valentine's Day or Easter. But I have not always done that with a great attitude. There have been moments when I've made a card with a scowl on my face. I've been grumpy. I've had a bad day. I've eaten the chocolate I got for her just because I could. Strike the angelic mom vision I almost tried to present. Just remember, celebrating our little ones is not always about being in a celebratory mood. Sometimes (many times), it's a choice we make—and as we are in the process of grumbling through our thanksgiving, we discover the smile that's been missing all day. It works.

So, my friends, take advantage of those little holidays throughout the year. Trust me, as I look at my teenager and wonder what happened to my preschooler, I have no regrets for the moments I celebrated. I have regrets about other things, but never about Valentine's ice cream or a card for Groundhog Day. It was those celebrations that made life and the subsequent memories sweet.

Have a monster bash. Celebrate birthdays. Let your child's birthday remind you of the miracle he or she is. I remember when Sami was just a newborn; I held her close, her head on my shoulder. It was late at night and I watched her fight sleep. Slowly her eyes closed and her little lips pursed as they suckled the air. She was magnificent, beautiful, incredible. I remember thinking to myself that I would never forget that moment. And I prayed—I hoped that in all my goofiness, in the moments that lay ahead, the toddler years, the preschool moments, the teenage years—that I would never forget what a miracle God had given me in her life.

And I haven't. I've made boatloads of mistakes, been frustrated when I meant to be calm, had grumpy moments when I haven't wanted to play or celebrate a single thing. But other times I get it. And I remember the miracle. It's one of the reasons I've always partied big on Sami's birthday. That's never meant I've spent a lot of money, but it has meant singing, a favorite meal, cards, cake, and people. It's a once-a-year gig and I figure it's worth some time and energy. I've had adults over, kids over; we've played games or danced all night. Whatever her little heart desires, as long as I can afford it and my body can keep up, I'm in. Why? Because she's alive. Because God gave her to me. Because if I don't celebrate her birthday, I just might forget how quickly the days pass. She'll be graduating from high school before I know it and how sad it would be if I hadn't danced all night or played Twister with little ones I could squish if I landed wrong. I'd hate to miss the giggles, the fun, and the pleasure in seeing her feel celebrated. Even if I can't put hours of planning into the perfect party, just like that one in the apartment complex so many years ago, I'm going to go for it. I'll tell you why: not only to remember and really see the beauty of my girl, but so that Sami will know she brings me joy.

Don't miss this. Kids need to know they bring us joy! They love knowing that who they are makes us smile. I once asked my mom, when I was all grown up, if I brought her joy when I was a little girl. I knew I was a handful; I knew I caused her a headache or two. But did I bring her joy? When she said, "Yes, of course," tears immediately came to my eyes. I didn't realize how important that was to me, to know that in the midst of the chaos, I brought her some good times as well. As single moms, it's easier to communicate the stress of parenting than the pleasure. But the pleasure matters, and our kids will notice whether or not we are glad they are in the world. Birthday parties give us the chance to do that.

Your Turn

Okay, I confess. There have been times when I've enjoyed feeling sorry for myself. It's true. For example, there have been more than a few years as a single parent when I deliberately chose not to tell anyone about my birthday. I told myself I just didn't want to make a fuss, but the truth is I kind of liked feeling sorry for myself as the day came and went without notice. Oh, someone would ask how I was doing on that day and I might slip it in, but that was only so they could join my pity party and feel sorry for me too. Besides, it really didn't feel right to organize my own birthday party, to find something to do for Valentine's Day, or to invite myself over to a sibling's house for Christmas. So different opportunities to celebrate came and went—and I used them to remind God and others that I was so completely, totally, horribly alone.

I've changed a bit since then.

This last birthday I invited all my friends over for a party. I asked them to bring food, big presents, and lots of laughter. Okay, I cut them some slack on the gifts—but I insisted on the food. We played games and I let them sing for me. I had a great time! Why feel sorry for myself when I can spend time with friends? Why not invite family to my home instead of whining about not being invited somewhere else? Sure, I could wait around for someone to remember my birthday, plan a party and include me. Or I could get angry that I've been forgotten or that no one thought how I might need a lift. But I can also believe the best about people in my world. I can realize they might be busy, even if they have the best of intentions. I can choose not to take it personally and plan something myself. I've tried both (feeling forgotten or choosing to celebrate myself), and I much prefer the latter. It's way more fun!

Really, as single moms with little ones, we have to take time to celebrate our own journeys. One of the hardest things about being single is not having someone to share in our accomplishments, joys, or special days. So we need to reach out and invite people to celebrate with us. If something good happens at work, call a friend. If your birthday is coming up, plan a party. If Valentine's Day is around the corner, call some girlfriends and schedule a girls' night.

This journey you're on takes effort. It takes all kinds of time, energy, and investment. So it's vitally important that you take moments to celebrate the good things that come your way: the promotion, the full night of rest, the meal that didn't turn cold before you had the chance to eat it. Big things, small things. Take a moment to savor the gift—celebrate!

Bottom line: There are always things to worry about. We can consume ourselves with taking care of the house, paying bills, disciplining, working, . . . the list goes on. So if we don't stop, take a few deep breaths, and recognize what is good, we'll miss out on the very things that make all those stressors worthwhile. Enjoy your children, enjoy your home, enjoy your friends. Celebrate your little one's laughter and take the time to celebrate the sweet accomplishments and special days in your own world. That way when you look back on this season of life, you'll recognize that while it's been hard, the memories created hold more than heartache—they hold joyous celebrations.

Additional Resources

Gaither, Gloria and Shirley Dobson. *Celebrating Special Times with Special People.*

Lansky, Vicki. *Birthday Parties: Best Party Tips and Ideas.*

Radic, Shelly. *The Birthday Book.*

Walker, Laura Jensen. *Girl Time: A Celebration of Chick Flicks, Bad Hair Days & Good Friends.*

Warner, Penny. *Kids' Party Games and Activities.*

8

Dreams

Amy watched as James furrowed his brow and put the final touches on his mansion. He'd used everything in the house, from toilet paper rolls to shoes and books. Amy's nice bowls were kidnapped for the pool and hot tub. (*Where did he learn about hot tubs?* she wondered.) A piece of green paper was meant to be the mini-golf course. Finally, he placed a rolled up sock on top of his new creation (for the watchtower) and turned to her.

"Mom?"

"Yes?"

"I want to build a big house someday."

Amy smiled. "You do?"

"Yes. A big house for us to live in. It'll have a really, really big staircase, an indoor basketball court, and a game room. Which," he paused as he looked at her, "I'll let you play in too. And we'll play in the pool and camp in the backyard and do all kinds of stuff. Okay?"

Amy nodded. "I bet you'll build awesome houses. Look at that; who wouldn't want to live in such a beautiful home? Look at that mini-golf course. How cool is that?"

James put his hands on his hips, puffed out his chest, and surveyed his creation. "Yes, I put the course in for me. I'm good at golf."

Again Amy nodded. "Yes, you are."

Moments later, the mansion was dismantled and James began his work on an indoor skate park—for kids only.

Amy continued to watch, her mind visualizing a grown-up version of her son working on blueprints for the world's next architectural masterpiece.

Dreams Matter

Kids love to dream. And they dream big. They dream about being pilots and doctors, skateboarders and professional football players. They imagine they will have lots of adventures, a fairy-tale wedding, and boatloads of kids. There are no limits, and at this age, why should there be? Sami, for a long time, wanted to be an astronaut, take care of animals, and fight fires. To combine the three, she decided that she would fly into space, doctor space creatures, and fight fires on the space station. She figured she could do them all.

It's fun for kids to dream, and as you encourage them, you will see their hearts delight in your belief. Are some of their dreams unreasonable? Yes, of course. While Sami probably could pull off the space veterinarian firefighter, I'm not altogether sure there will be space creatures available to nurse back to health. Even so, I cheered her desire, and I loved watching her eyes light up. Honoring her dreams mattered to her.

So what does it look like to encourage our kids in real ways? Maybe some of these things will help.

Let them dream big. Okay, the likelihood of your tyke going out for the NFL, flying into space, or dancing her way to stardom may not be huge. But letting him or her dream, and encouraging those dreams, is a wonderful gift. And besides, you never know, someone has to end up in the NFL, someone has to be president of the United States; why not your little one?

Let them dream their own dreams. I was doing my weekly swim at the pool the other day when I noticed a mom and her two daughters. The older daughter seemed to love swimming and was doing her laps with energy and enthusiasm. The younger daughter, about four or five years old, had absolutely no interest in swimming the length of the pool. She could do it, she had the skill, but when she got to the other end, her greater interest was in counting the number of plastic rings separating the lanes.

I overheard her mom chastising her. "Don't you want to be a racer, Lisa? Come on, swim back to Mom!"

I caught the little girl's eye as I came closer. She scrunched up her face, puffed out her lips, and stuck her little pink tongue out at me. I couldn't help but grin at her. I knew the look wasn't for me but for her mom. She didn't want to be a racer, she wanted to count plastic rings. It was her mom who wanted her to be a racer.

Sometimes, in our desire for our kids to know success, we'll start them at a tender age in the hobby/sport/music of our choosing. These things are good, but when they are driven more by *our* dreams than our preschooler's dreams, it's time to take a step back and let them count some rings.

Encourage natural strengths. Sami was born creative. She liked to hear stories, tell stories, read, draw, color, and act things out. She was never very interested in basketball or other sports. She preferred stuffed animals over dolls, and relationships over being alone. Over the years, it's been fun to encourage her specific wiring. I remember stories she's told about rubber dinosaurs and red-headed ants, puppy dog giggles and ice-cream robbers. In the midst of those stories, she (still) loves to make me laugh. Knowing that, I laugh all the more. Knowing she is relational, I love to connect her with friends and cousins, and her love for animals meant cats and dogs were adopted into our family (along with piles of the stuffed variety now long forgotten and heaped in the garage).

Whatever your child enjoys, celebrate that with him or her. If he's really into building things, delight in his creations, even when you're not sure what they are. If she's good with a nerf football, play catch with her and teach her to throw a spiral. Whatever your children love and show interest in, give them encouragement and enjoy their gifts and strengths. We'll talk about that even more in a later chapter.

Foster realistic dreams. Sometimes kids dream big dreams—but they have to do with bringing the family back together. They want Dad under their roof, they want to be a family again, they want all of you to live happily ever after. These are harder dreams to hear and harder ones to handle. You don't necessarily want to get into a long discussion about the impossibility of Dad being around, but you don't want your child clinging to a dream that's not realistic.

If your children are constantly dreaming of a reunited family, it's okay to let them know it won't happen. You can scoop them up, hold them close, and say something like: "I'm sorry, honey; I know you want to see Mommy and Daddy at the same time, but we don't live in the same place anymore. Why don't we give your dad a call and you can say hello." If they are connected to their dad, this would be ideal. If their dad isn't in the picture at all, through death or abandonment, then scoop them up, hold them close, and let them know that Dad won't be back—and that it's okay to be sad. Then remind them that you are still a family, that God has you in his hand, and that it's okay to dream new dreams.

Your child may include his or her dad in a dream of the future as a peripheral person. Maybe Dad is just part of the story, but the focus of the story is the child's dream and the adventures that will follow. In that case, you don't need to go to the deep places and remind them Dad won't be there.

Your Turn

I had it planned. I would meet the perfect man when I was twenty-two years old, we'd marry and begin having children—five altogether. On the side I would be a best-selling author, the female version of Jacques Cousteau, and a worldwide traveler. My husband would be handsome and charming, I would be svelte and engaging. Life would be sweet.

I wasn't real happy to find myself, at twenty-four, working to survive as a waitress in a local restaurant/bar. I was divorced and the single mom of a toddler. The closest I came to scuba diving was soaking in the bathtub, and my best writing was done as I described the type of meat my customers ordered ("magnificently rare"; "superbly well done"; "delectably raw"). My dreams were about as far from reality as could be.

If you're anything like me, your dreams may have been shelved by the realities of divorce, death, or heartache. Maybe you're tired of dreaming dreams because none of them ever seem to come true. Or maybe you feel disqualified because of the circumstances that now surround your life. If so, please hear me. Your dreams still matter. Maybe they won't come true in the way you initially planned, but you don't have to give up on them. You need hope for your future as well. It will help as you walk through some of the tougher todays. Here are some practical ways to nurture your own dreams.

Get to know God. God is the biggest dreamer of all. It's amazing how he can use all of our broken pieces, heartaches, and poor choices, craft them together with his love, and give us hope beyond our imagination. As I got to know and love God, he seemed to take those dreams (which I'd stuffed beyond reach) and resurrect them with his kindness. I was able to write—not just about cheesy stuff that didn't make much of a difference but about the real ways God reaches out to people like you and me. I was able to travel—as a single mom he allowed me to go places that I could never afford without his help. I didn't have five kids, but I discovered this wonderful opportunity to love and invest in my nephews and nieces. God took away some of my bitterness and invited himself to my huge pity party. As he brought people into my world who loved me, and as I started going to church and getting involved in community, he showed me his heart. Which was much kinder and more real in its love than I ever imagined it to be. Get to know and love God; it changes everything.

Think about what you would like to do someday. Your children are going to grow up. As they grow older, you'll have more freedom and more opportunities to expand your own world. So what does that look like for you? Do you want to be a teacher? Writer? Computer guru? Do you want to live by the ocean? Near a mountain?

I remember being absolutely stumped. I knew what I'd dreamed of as a child, but what did I want for my future? What did that look like? I knew I wanted to write, and I knew I wanted to do something with people, but what else? I used to take on other people's dreams. I took on what I thought my parents wanted and what my husband hoped for, but what did I want? I remember thinking about what kind of home I would like. I decided I wanted a small place on a lake—a place where I could walk outside and have a cup of coffee as I looked over the water. I didn't want a big or fancy place, just a nice comfy home where I could write, fish, and have people over without worrying about where or how things might spill. It was fun to think and dream about that home.

Surround yourself with "Yes" folks. I hung around lots of "No" people early on in my divorce. You know who I'm talking about—the folks who can't seem to move past today. The ones who don't want to see you dreaming big dreams because they've given up completely. Do whatever you can to associate with people who will believe in you and encourage you. Take steps to believe in those around you. Become a "Yes" person even as you surround yourself with "Yes" people. The game isn't over; there's more to the future than you can begin to imagine. I've met so many folks in their twenties and thirties who have determined life as they know it is over. It's simply not true. Passion and hope can be contagious. Do what you can to be with people who are contagious in their love for God and their belief in you. As you experience that same love, you'll become more and more a "Yes" person, for yourself and for those around you.

Learn to forgive. One of the biggest hurdles for me in dreaming again was learning to forgive. I was mad at the injustice of the world (and how that played out in my own particular story), and I was mad at myself. How could I dream again? So-and-so ruined my dreams. And besides, I didn't deserve to dream; didn't anyone notice how I had messed everything up? I was stuck in that place for a long time. I didn't want to forgive anyone else, and I didn't know how to forgive myself. But I had to if I was ever going to move forward.

Forgiving others is all about choosing to release them from the debt they owe you. It is not an invitation for them to hurt you again. Forgiveness is saying that you no longer expect or need for them to make it right. You are choosing to let it go. That process can be a long one, which we'll discuss more in a later chapter. But know this: forgiveness is something that needs to happen in order for our dreams to grow. Without it, we tend to keep looking back and have difficulty dreaming forward.

I was good at sabotaging my own dreams. I didn't think I deserved any happiness so I made sure I didn't experience it too often. I'm not sure when exactly it happened, but slowly (through friends and Scripture) I began to realize that sabotaging my life didn't serve anyone. It didn't serve God, my parents, or my daughter. How much better it was when I finally decided to receive the gift of forgiveness that God offered me! How much better

I served him when I looked at folks in my world with a smile on my face—when I chased after my dreams and accepted that, even though I may not have done everything right, God still might have a future for me.

We always serve God best by accepting the gift of forgiveness and by moving forward with joy—think of it! It is in our joy that we will bless our family and friends, and delight our God, because others will naturally be drawn to the One who saved us. We're not a very good witness if our head is hung low.

Bottom line: Let your little ones dream. Especially on the harder days when you're all needing a dose of hope, dream about what they would love to do someday. Imagine together what they will be when they're all "grown up." Have fun with it. And begin dreaming again for yourself. There's so much ahead of you, so much joy to grab hold of. You are wired for a very specific hope and future; give yourself the freedom to dream. God has much in mind for you!

Additional Resources

Eldredge, John. *Dare to Desire: An Invitation to Fulfill Your Deepest Dreams.*

Jaynes, Sharon. *Dreams of a Woman: God's Plan for Fulfilling Your Dreams.*

Maxwell, John C. *The Success Journey: The Process of Living Your Dreams.*

Warren, Rick. *The Purpose-Driven Life.*

Wilkinson, Bruce. *The Dream Giver.*

9

Cuddles and Touch

Every Tuesday evening I meet with Lauriza. She teases me, comparing our time to the now-famous book *Tuesdays with Morrie*. "It's *Tuesday with Elsa*," she says. Which, if you ask me, doesn't sound anywhere near as catchy.

Usually when Lauriza and I meet, it's just the two of us. But this last Tuesday, Lanie, her preschooler, begged to come along. "It's just going to be boring conversation," Lauriza had told her (not sure how I felt about that). "Why don't you stay with your aunties?"

"I don't care, Mom," Lanie insisted. "I want to come! I want to go to Elsa's!" So under strict guidelines that Lanie be still, Lauriza allowed her to come.

It didn't take long to see what Lanie was up to. She didn't come over to see me. She didn't come for the invigorating conversation. She came so she could curl up with her mom. Within fifteen minutes of their arrival,

Lanie nestled herself into her mom's arms and promptly fell asleep. She stayed that way, tucked in close, until it was time to leave. She just wanted her mom. No frills. No play. No conversation. Just the touch of Mom holding her close and keeping her safe.

And so it is with our preschoolers. Some may express it just like Lanie, curling up when they need touch and connection. Others run wild and have a hard time sitting still long enough for a quick hug. Yet no matter how they are wired, every preschooler needs touch. Whether it's a passing high five, a quick hug, or a marathon cuddle session while watching cartoons—each one is hardwired and has a God-given need for touch and physical connection.

Cuddles Matter

Your Child's Need for Touch

Jan is the single mom of three young boys. Her husband died in a car accident, leaving her to raise Josh (four), Jason (six), and Alex (eight). Her world went from caring for the boys at home with the help of a supportive husband to working a part-time job while trying to manage her home and family on her own. Everything was different. To compound the problem, her youngest seemed especially terrified to leave her side. He wanted to sleep with her, cuddle close, and cling to her hand. He was afraid he might lose her too.

Jan's story isn't unusual. Whether you're never married, divorced, or widowed, your child has experienced some type of loss that makes the need for touch and connection even more critical. It can seem overwhelming though, to try to work in time to sit and hold your kids while taking care of everything else that comes your way. Try some of these ideas to increase touch time without spending every evening curled up on the couch with your little ones.

Holding hands. Anytime Jan walked with the kids, they held hands. She told them it was for safety (and partly it was), but it also gave them the chance to touch. She encouraged Alex to hold Josh's hand and reminded him of his special role as big brother. Allowing the kids to hold hands with each other gave them time to connect as well.

Wrestling/tickling. For the more active preschooler, this may be the only touch they'll receive. They may not like holding hands, cuddling, or hugging—but a good wrestling match, that's a different story! Wrestling is a good thing. It not only gives your child the chance to get rid of some energy, it might be a great thing for you to get rid of some as well.

Hugs and kisses. Whenever possible, send your children off to preschool and welcome them home with hugs and kisses. Just make it part of your routine. Even when you're feeling overwhelmed, take a moment to smile, hold them close, and let them know you're glad to see them. A warm hug communicates volumes.

Couch time. Another single mom friend of mine has "couch time." In addition to hugs and high fives throughout the week, Saturday morning is couch time, when she and her two girls watch cartoons for an hour. By scheduling the time, she makes sure it happens. "Otherwise," she says, "two weeks will pass without any touch time at all."

What to Avoid

Some parents choose to get some cuddle time in by allowing their preschooler to sleep with them. While this may seem like a great solution, there are definite drawbacks. What happens if you eventually marry? Not only will your child have to work through including someone else in the family, but he or she will also lose that precious place beside Mom in bed. Allowing your child to sleep in the same bed opens the door to all kinds of other frustrations as well—for example, at what point will that change? Some parents think they'll allow it until their child is "ready" to sleep on their own. But how do you gauge that? And what do you do if your child is thirteen and afraid to spend the night on his or her own? Yes, cuddling is definitely important, but avoid having your child sleep in bed with you.

If you're already doing that, go ahead and transition them into their own bed. Cuddle with them for a few minutes there and then separate. They won't like it at first, but stand firm.

It could also be you enjoy having your child sleep with you; the transition will be tough for you as well. Maybe sleeping in the same bed has eased some of your loneliness. Understandable. But there are other ways to meet that need (we'll talk about those a little later in the chapter). For now, know that it's not good for you to fill that need with your child—it makes it harder for them to grow to independence in the way that they should, and they may take on too much responsibility for your emotions and lean toward codependency as they get older.

Here's a final thought: you could be one of the fortunate ones who has a child wired in similar ways to you. He could be a cuddler, and maybe you are too. So it works out well to curl up on the couch for a few minutes every evening. For most of us though, there's a difference. Our kids need more than we feel we can offer, or they need us less than we'd like. Whatever the case, do your best to take the time to greet them warmly, hold them close, and communicate your love consistently through physical touch.

Your Turn

I couldn't help but be embarrassed. There I was, on the massage table, getting my very first massage ever. I'd received a gift certificate for my birthday and was on this table facedown as the young therapist rubbed my back and shoulders. But it had been such a long time since I'd been touched by anyone that as she massaged the muscles in my shoulders, tears slipped from my closed eyes and fell to the floor. I couldn't help it. The touch itself reminded me of how lonely I'd been for physical contact. I was grieving even as I was soaking in the sweetness of it. She asked me to turn over so she could massage my arms. When she saw the tears, she was worried. "Oh my, did I hurt you?"

"No," I mumbled, wiping them away. "It just feels very nice."

I don't know what she must have thought. Or maybe she didn't think anything of it. My guess is, she'd seen lots of lonely folks and I probably wasn't the first to react emotionally to the touch. Maybe she understood more than I knew.

Our Need for Touch

As single moms, we need touch. We need connection with other human beings. And while cuddling with our kids is helpful, they can't be the ones to meet our primary need. It's like we talked about earlier; that can put too much pressure on our kids. Of course, if you're anything like me, you may not even acknowledge the need for touch. It may feel frivolous or somehow not as important as all the other needs calling out to us. Unfortunately, if we don't acknowledge the need, it can sneak up and cause us to make some choices that might not be wise. Sometimes, acknowledging a need is the first step toward protecting us from a bad choice. Then, at least, we can take some steps to enjoy healthy interaction.

So what does receiving some healthy touch look like? Let's look at a few practical ways we can meet the need.

Try hugging. I loved the women's ministry at our church. When I first walked through their doors, I looked at them a little crosswise. I couldn't imagine a married woman of three would have anything to say to a single parent of one. I was pretty critical actually, thinking they had no clue what my life was like and probably didn't care to find out. But as I kept showing up, as I got to know them, I discovered the most amazing thing: they weren't all that different from me. They were women who were frustrated by different circumstances, thrilled by others, excited about the future, or heartbroken about the past. I even discovered some of the married women were actually single parents. Their husbands were so far removed or so distant they were parenting on their own anyway. I was amazed to discover that married or single, parent or not, they had a lot of the same needs I did—including safe and healthy touch. When I first showed up at that ministry, I wasn't real big on hugging these church ladies who seemed so different from me. But before long

I learned that something in those hugs filled something in me. I needed them. I needed to know that someone was glad to see me. I needed to feel like I belonged. Pretty soon, as I began to build relationships and really get to know the women, I was hugging them as I walked in and hugging them as I walked out. I loved it!

If you can, get involved in a women's group, whether it's through MOPS, a small group in your home, or the women's ministry at your church. You are not the only one longing for healthy connection. Give other women the opportunity to encourage you with their kindness and touch. And no, you won't hit it off with everyone, but if you open the door and reach out, you will definitely meet up with one or two women who will offer those sweet hugs after a class together.

Treat yourself to a massage. If I could, I'd have a massage every week. I don't. I don't have the money and I don't have the time. But when I have had the opportunity, it's done me a world of good. Initially, I wondered if it was okay to get a massage—should I even do that? But once I discovered that doctors recommend and encourage it, that it has all kinds of health benefits, and there are reputable places, I decided to go for it. Of course, I couldn't afford a super fancy spa, but I've asked around and found out about other options. Some colleges offer massage therapy and will look for guinea pigs for their students to practice on. Make sure it's a reputable school, but such an arrangement could keep the cost down. Also, check with your doctor. He or she may know of an upstanding massage therapist with reasonable rates. It really does help our physical and mental well-being to get some of those kinks worked out. The biggest obstacle is usually cost, so think about asking for a massage for

Christmas or as a birthday gift from friends or relatives. It's definitely worth it!

Build close friendships. My dearest friend and accountability partner is a mother of five. We've been friends for years. We don't live near each other anymore, but when we did I often went over to her home on Saturday morning. Her husband worked on the house, the kids played together, and we talked about all kinds of things. We took turns on alternating visits rubbing each other's shoulders, and at the end of our time, we'd always close by holding hands and praying for each other. It was awesome—good, healthy connection that offered sweet, safe touch. We need that! We'll talk about it more in a later chapter, but do what you can to invest in at least one solid, female friendship. That will be another avenue to experience safe touch.

What to Avoid

The danger in not giving yourself the freedom to touch in healthy ways is that the need for touch will surface in the most unexpected (and often unhealthy) ways. I can remember when Sami was just a little girl; I was invited out with some friends. A local band was playing and we thought it might be fun to dance. At one point, a guy asked me to dance and I said yes. I didn't know him but found myself hoping he would ask for a slow dance. I wanted him to hold me; I wanted to feel a strong hand on my back and a body close to mine. I was surprised by the need; it caught me off guard, and if I hadn't been with friends who knew to pull me away, I would have gone for the touch without wanting to think about the potential consequences.

I know the desire. You are not alone in that; I just encourage you to seek out healthy ways to give and receive affection. Don't settle by sacrificing your convictions or what you know to be right to experience the touch of another. Understand the need is present and then give yourself healthy avenues to meet it. It's worth it to make healthy touch a priority in your world.

Bottom line: Both you and your children need touch. Hold each other, hug friends, treat yourself to a massage. Take appropriate steps and find safe avenues to experience connection with others. It's worth the effort!

Additional Resources

Dillow, Linda, and Lorraine Pintus. *Intimate Issues.*

Elliot, Elisabeth. *Passion and Purity.*

Ethridge, Shannon. *Every Woman's Battle.*

Osborne, Rick. *Parenting at the Speed of Life: 60 Ways to Capture Time With Your Kids.*

Part 3

Here's to Your Health

10

Rest

I call them meltdowns. Sami has them, I have them, and they're never pretty. Both Sami and I are very expressive. There's little doubt what either one of us is feeling at any given moment. When we're both tired, things can get ugly.

One particular Monday morning comes to mind when Sami was about four years old. We'd been up late the night before, spending time at a friend's house. Morning came too quickly, and we were in a rush to get ready for preschool and work. Sami was usually pretty good at dressing herself, but on this occasion, she chose not to wear what I set out and went instead for plaid pants and a polka-dot shirt. The whole ensemble really worked in her mind, and to add a little spice to her getup, she also asked for pigtails done up in different colored scrunchies.

No offense to anyone who enjoys the unique combination of plaid and polka dots, but I didn't like it.

"Sami, put on the shirt I laid out, please."

"I don't want to!"

"Do it now, Sami, we need to go."

"But I like this shirt! It's prettier than that other one!"

"No, it's not. What you're wearing doesn't match. Put on the other one."

"NO!!!" she yelled, as she stomped her foot. "I look good!!"

I was tired. Sami was tired. What should have followed was a quick correction of her disrespect, a little grace for her fashion statement, and a loving hug—a Hallmark moment wrapped up in sound parenting.

It didn't happen.

Instead, what followed was a four-year-old undoing a twenty-something-year-old. I didn't want to deal with it and stomped off. She stomped into her room and fell dramatically onto her bed in a fit of tears. I slammed my door, highlighting my immaturity, and she howled louder in response.

All over plaid pants and a polka-dot shirt.

Needless to say, I was late for work that day. I was grumpy and irritated, and I'm certain that Sami was no better as her attitude spilled out at preschool. Looking back now, I can tie that morning (and others like it) to lack of rest. I don't respond well when I haven't had enough sleep. Neither does Sami. We're more irritated, quick to fall apart, and tend toward the dramatic. Add in some stress—a problem at school or work, or a financial mishap—and you might as well call in some boxing referees and ESPN; there's going to be a showdown.

Sleep Matters

It's relatively easy to find research that talks about the value of sleep. We need it. When we don't have it, we perform at less than our best. An article in the November 2003 issue of *Scientific American* discusses how lack of sleep can impair our responses in a way similar to drinking too much alcohol. In other words, without sleep, we get loopy.

This goes for our kids too. When they don't get the rest they need, they have a harder time learning, obeying, and connecting to others. Plus, their bodies need extra sleep as they grow. According to research, most preschoolers should get between ten and twelve hours of sleep per day. In addition to growing, their bodies need the time to recuperate and reenergize from the day before. Without that sleep, they are more prone to illness, irritability, and distraction. Sound familiar?

So, you may think, *that's wonderful, but how exactly are we supposed to get enough sleep? There's too much to do!* I understand that completely! When I fall into bed at 11:30 p.m. and set my alarm for 5:30 a.m.—and still have too much to do—I wonder how I am supposed to pack in a full eight hours of rest. It just isn't possible! And trying to get Sami in bed by a reasonable hour has never been a simple task either. When she was a preschooler, just being home at 8:00 p.m. was a feat in itself, much less getting her bathed and to sleep!

With adequate sleep, you (and your kids) will be in better shape to handle whatever stressors might come your way. So what baby steps can you take to incorporate more rest into the day? Let's start with the kids.

Rest for the Wild Ones

Stick to a scheduled bedtime with a routine. When Sami was a preschooler, she knew that after dinner was bath time, then story, then bed. We weren't always able to keep our routine, but it helped her (and me) when we did. Besides, since we had to be up early we had to be in bed by 7:30 or 8:00 to get enough sleep. Sure, setting that schedule meant I couldn't go out and about very often—but honestly, I didn't really *need* to.

A schedule really worked for Sami—when she was well rested, the world was a much brighter place. Rest can work for your children as well. Single parenthood is stressful enough without throwing in lack of sleep! Make sure your kids go to bed on time.

Incorporate quiet time. I learned this from my sister-in-law, Carol. Every day after lunch, she would tell her three kids to climb into their beds for an hour of quiet time. Whether they were at an age to nap or not, they had to go to their beds and be still (read, color, relax) for an hour. Granted, most of you work throughout the week, so it's not really an issue. But you can still incorporate a quiet time into your weekends—it will give your kids a chance to rest and give you the chance as well.

I had quiet times with Sami until she was ten years old. She didn't really need them any longer, but I still loved them. "But, Mom!" she would whine. "I'm too old; I don't need a nap." I stayed firm. "I know, honey, and I'm too young to take a nap. But we're going to enjoy some quiet anyway." It was good for both of us to have a little downtime, especially in the middle of a busy weekend day.

Enjoy cuddle time. Sami loved to cuddle, so this worked well in our home. She would curl up next to me, and we'd put on a cute cartoon. She'd watch; I'd rest. And both of us had the chance to relax. Granted, some of you have a child like my friend Anna's. Her son will have nothing to do with cuddling. He travels at 90 mph all day long and the thought of sitting still, curled up with his mommy, has no appeal. I wish I had something wise and motherly to say in that scenario. I don't. Anna still curls up on the couch, but Nathanial doesn't slow down. So Anna will get him focused on crashing cars around the living room floor (with something close to an inside voice) so she can watch and still lie down. And since her son isn't actually running at normal speed, it ends up being a rest time for him as well.

Your Turn

Keep a schedule. Put your child in bed, but make sure you are able to get to bed on time as well. Commit to yourself that you will go to sleep by a certain hour. Try to get at least seven hours of sleep per night. The experts recommend eight—but I know the likelihood of that for any one of us. If you can get at least seven, you'll feel better during the day.

Take catnaps. This would be a good time to confess something. Today, as I was writing this very chapter, my head began to nod. Sitting at my desk, writing about rest, I was nodding off. I couldn't help it—it's been a long day. So what I tried to do is not look too much like I was sleeping. I sat straight up in my cubicle (I'm writing this book on weekends, over my lunch hour, and in the early mornings at my regular workplace), and faced the computer. Then I closed my eyes. I hoped my head wouldn't dip or that a snore wouldn't escape, but I went for it anyway. See, I'm still a single mother. My daughter is thirteen, but I still deal with many of the same issues that I did when Sami was a preschooler. I get tired during the day, and sometimes a catnap is just what I need.

Today, I slept sitting up for ten minutes. I feel a lot better (though I confess, I'm about ready for another one). So if you can, take a little rest where you can grab it. Naps are a good thing.

Know what to let go of. I have a friend, a single mom of a preschooler, who is trying to fulfill all her dreams in one year. She's working hard at her job, going to school, taking on some additional job training, dating a nice guy, and taking care of her home—in addition to being a single mom of a beautiful little girl. I get tired just thinking about all that she has on her plate! All her goals are good things—she's going to school to get a better job, she's working hard to further her career, she's taking care of details so her home won't fall apart. But she hardly gets any sleep—and by the time the weekend starts, her best hope is to get in a short nap, work on some homework, and hopefully spend time with her daughter. It's exhausting, and her lack of sleep spills out and affects every other area of her life.

So how do we, as single moms, determine what we should hold on to? And what we should let go of? And finally, how do we get some sleep in the middle of it all?

Try this. When all your options are good, it's time to think about what is best. You need God. You need your family. You need your job to provide for your family. You need friendships and community to keep you grounded in good counsel. But beyond that, what else matters? You are the one who has to discern what you can do with the time you have. I was recently asked to write a workbook for a publisher. I really wanted to do it because it falls in line with my passion and it would provide some additional income. But it would have meant a horrible rush through the holiday season. The deadline was short, and I would have to cut my time with Sami. One of my dear friends put a bug in my ear: "Elsa, honey, you *can* say no." I guess I knew that, somewhere in my heart. But hearing it from her helped. I *could* say no. I needed the money, but I needed my daughter and my rest more.

Thinking back on the past few months, I'm so glad I did say no. I would have been miserable trying to complete a workbook through the busy holiday season we just experienced.

Take a few minutes and think about where you are investing your time. Is there something you can cut out of your schedule so you can get more rest? You don't have to do everything during this time in life. Your children will grow older, and you'll have some other opportunities to do those less pressing things. With some more rest and focused time, you'll discover you're better able to enjoy the sweet moments of parenting. You'll laugh more, engage with your kids, and have more energy.

Think about it. If you have trouble thinking of anything, talk to a close friend. Ask what she thinks of your priorities and if there is a place you can trim things down. Sometimes other people have better insight into our lives than we do. Once you get some counsel, take immediate steps to follow through. You have a tough job—you need your rest.

In fact, think of me as your mom. I look at you with worried eyes, notice you're a little pale around the gills, and send you off to bed. "Go get some rest, honey. You need it right now. We'll talk more soon."

Bottom line: Your children need rest. You need rest. With a good sleep, you'll both be better equipped to wake up and face the day with a smile. While it might be difficult to schedule rest into your day, make it a priority. Even the toughest scenarios, those wrapped around plaid and polka dots, will be better handled with a rested perspective.

Additional Resources

Aldrich, Sandra. *From One Single Mother to Another: Heart-Lifting Encouragement and Practical Advice.*

Hager, W. David, and Linda Carruth Hager. *Stress and the Woman's Body.*

Koole, Richard. *Outsmarting Stress: Biblical Principles for Handling Life's Pressures.*

Swenson, Richard A. *The Overload Syndrome: Learning to Live Within Your Limits.*

Trent, John. *Bedtime Blessings, Volume 2: 100 Bedtime Stories and Activities for Blessing Your Child.*

11

Nutrition

Kathy stared at the full plates sitting on the table. Chicken, corn, mashed potatoes—one of the better meals she'd prepared of late. Two bites were missing from Jonathan's plate, three from Maureen's, and five from her own. She'd been so excited too. Just recently, they'd welcomed in the New Year, and Kathy had committed to a fast from corn dogs and macaroni and cheese. No more pizza slices and microwavable burritos with mysterious fillers. She was going to cook hearty, healthy meals if it killed her.

And she was thinking it just might.

But healthy meals weren't even the whole problem. By the time the family did sit down, no one was hungry. Because she and the kids came home from after-school care and work at 5:30, all of them were usually "starving" for something to eat. Snacks meant to tide them to dinnertime usually filled them all the way up. So whether healthy or unhealthy, dinner didn't hold much appeal.

Then, by the time bedtime rolled around, Jonathan always needed something else and Maureen cried if she didn't have a little snack. ("But my tummy is all empty; it needs something big!")

Kathy was frustrated. She wanted the kids to eat healthy, but pulling it off always seemed just out of reach. And her own diet? She had great aspirations to obediently follow the food pyramid gurus and eat her daily servings of fruit and vegetables, but that wasn't happening either. In fact, the pyramid people would probably flog her with fiber if they only knew how pitifully she followed their guidelines.

What was the use?

Nutrition Matters

If you've ever felt like Kathy, you should remember that nutrition does matter. While we won't get it right all the time, it is definitely worth the effort to feed our kids good food. We'll talk about our own healthy choices a little later in the chapter, but let's start with some motivators to fight the good fight with our kids.

Feed their bodies. Our kids are growing. Their bodies are growing taller, their muscles are growing stronger, their bones are lengthening. They're in need of good food to help the process, to give them all they need to develop physically.

Feed their minds. You've heard it—brain food. There are definitely certain types of foods that will help our kids to concentrate better. We all know that sugar will send our kids bouncing off the walls physically, but that same hyperactivity will also impair their ability to think and focus. In this season of life, when they desperately need to focus and learn, limiting their sugar intake and increasing healthy foods is imperative.

Stem obesity. It's all over the news these days: because kids are less active and are eating more, they're dealing with obesity at younger and younger ages. Obesity is not only a danger health-wise, it also affects a child's self-esteem. We must train our kids early about the value of fruits, veggies, and reasonable portion sizes.

Make healthy choices for sanity's sake. Junk food has its effects on our kids' behavior. Give a child a Coke and a candy bar and you know exactly what I'm talking about. We need to opt for healthy choices not only to help our kids grow physically and mentally but also to minimize our own frustrations in dealing with kids who haven't eaten well and whose behavior reflects it.

Fight illness. Without good nutrition, our kids will be much more prone to the illnesses they encounter in preschool, Sunday school, or at the playground. By giving them a good balance of healthy foods, we'll be better able to help them resist the illness that little Bobby-Jo might willingly pass on through goobery kisses.

What You Can Do

You don't have to be a master chef or grow your own garden to get some decent food into your kids' bodies. Try some of these techniques to ease the process.

Always have salad. My friend Jane makes a big salad without dressing about twice a week and sticks it in the refrigerator. Then she puts a little bit beside whatever meal they're having and voila! Greens. The kids know to expect it, and while they fussed at the beginning, they know it's not an option—and they can't get up from the table unless they eat at least a few bites.

Munch on healthy snacks. If you are tempted to eat as soon as you walk in the door, grab some healthy bite-sized snacks. Little carrots are wonderful—full of good nutrients and sweet to taste. Grapes are another quick-grab snack, along with strawberries, apples, or oranges.

Hide veggies in meals. My daughter always liked tacos—a great way to sneak in some lettuce and tomatoes. Soups and stews are other opportunities to get a few veggies into your unsuspecting little one. Although "live" veggies (uncooked) are best nutrition-wise, sometimes you'll have to do the best with what you have.

Avoid late-night snacking. My friend Jennifer has a little sign she posts over the kitchen at 7:00 p.m. It reads, "Kitchen Closed!" It took some getting used to, but once her kids realized they weren't allowed anything to eat after 7:00, they were more interested in finishing their dinners and grabbing an early snack.

Encourage fast-food health. If you occasionally eat out for fast food (or even if it's more than occasionally), take advantage of the menus that offer healthy alternatives to french fries. A number of places will now allow you to substitute salad or fresh fruit.

Model small portions. For yourself, don't eat more than you need. Kids will model what they eat after your choices. If they see a "grown-up" portion as much larger, that's what they'll aspire to. Take just a small portion, then if you're still hungry, take a bit more.

Make "fun" food. If you check on the Internet and plug in "healthy fun snacks," you'll discover a number of websites with some neat recipes to encourage your kids to have fun with good foods: strawberry popsicles, veggie sticks—different items that are fun to make and fun to eat.

Remember, if you only incorporate one or two of the above ideas into your schedule, you will already be ahead of where you've been. And that's the key; expecting yourself to change your eating lifestyle overnight will be altogether too stressful. Do what you can and keep your eyes open for opportunities to introduce healthy foods into your family's diet.

Your Turn

Laura was concerned about giving her young son good food. She made sure he ate a healthy breakfast; she packed him nice little lunches with grapes and celery sticks and did her best to get a few pieces of salad into him every night. Her own nutrition? She didn't see much point in worrying about that. It just wasn't very high on her priority list—until she ended up at the doctor's office with a stern young doctor eyeing her over her test results. "You have low iron," he said. "How's your diet?"

Laura thought about donuts grabbed on the run, quick sandwiches, and gourmet vending items—no wonder she was so tired all the time. Her body was depleted of iron, and for some odd reason, strawberry donuts weren't doing the trick.

She hung her head. "It's okay, I guess."

Fifteen minutes later, she left with a list of iron-rich foods and her doctor's lecture ringing in her ears. Her food choices mattered. And if she didn't make better choices, she'd have to deal with the consequences of her own limited energy.

I completely resonate with Laura. I've always been low on iron, and I've always struggled to stay on top of my own health and nutrition. But good nutrition does matter for us as single moms.

Here are a few benefits to help you stay the course:

- *More energy.* As we eat foods that offer the right nutrients, our bodies will have more energy. As single moms, we're already fighting an uphill battle to stay ahead of the game. By feeding our body well, we'll have the energy to take care of our kids and our home.
- *Ability to fight off illness.* We don't have time to be sick. Granted, there are times we can't avoid the germs that crowd around at the office or in our home, but we can set ourselves up to be as resistant as possible. If we're eating well, getting all that yummy vitamin C, E, and D, we'll be better able to battle the viruses that sneeze through our world.
- *Better attitude.* Ever get the grumpies after a junk food binge? There really is such a thing as a sugar crash. If we pump sugar into our systems for that high, we'll also get the low that follows. By maintaining a healthy diet, minus the mass-infusions of caffeine or sugar, we'll be better able to stay focused and maintain a positive attitude.
- *Healthy self-image.* I can't stand when my pants are tight. I don't like when I've eaten too much junk and I feel it in my clothes. That alone will put me in a mood to grouch at whoever happens by. By maintaining a healthy diet, I feel better about myself. I may not like eating rabbit food, but I always feel good about the decision afterward.

- *Better sleep.* Too much junk food affects our sleep. Like sugar highs and crashes, if we dump lousy stuff into our system, it will affect our rest. Or, if we eat right before bed, it will upset our sleep, give us odd dreams, or cause restlessness.
- *Fewer zits.* You've heard it—too much chocolate and too much grease will affect your complexion. And really, with all the other stuff going on in our world, who needs pimples?

Okay, so now you're inspired to be energetic, healthy, zit-free single moms. Now we can move to some of the practical tools that will help get you there.

Check the Internet. I'm amazed at how much information you can gather on the Internet. We talked about it for healthy kids' snacks, but if you plug "healthy recipes" into your search engine, you should come up with a number of sites that will help you with grown-up stuff as well. I'm not big on cooking, so I need stuff with few ingredients and a limited number of exotic spices. I have the basics (salt, pepper, garlic) and need to stick with those. It's possible. There are sites with four-ingredient meals, seven-ingredient meals, and more. You can find soup recipes, casseroles—whatever best suits your kitchen, your supplies, and your needs.

Always make too much. If you make a meal, make sure you pack leftovers for lunch the next day. This will keep you from grabbing something quick and unhealthy. It'll definitely save money as well.

Pack healthy snacks you enjoy. I'm usually hungry by 3:00 p.m. If nothing's around, I'll make a run to the vending machine and go for the cheese curls. I love cheese curls—the crunchy ones. Those and Hershey bars with almonds. Yeah, not exactly healthy fare. So I've started packing apples and raw almonds. I used to pack carrots, but despite what I said earlier about how good they are, I think they're gross. I'd pack 'em with the best of intentions and never eat one. Make sure you pack healthy snacks that you'll actually eat.

Eat breakfast. Everyone always says to eat breakfast, so I'm just joining the bandwagon. I know how hard it is to get your kids ready and still grab a bite to eat. Most days, I don't get to breakfast myself, so I can't (in good conscience) push this one too hard. If you can, try to have some cereal, oatmeal, fruit, or a muffin. Get something in you so you're not tempted to go the unhealthy route mid-morning.

Eat lots of grains, fruits, and veggies. Again, go for stuff you like. Maybe, like when cooking for your kids, you need to hide it in different dishes. Do what you have to do. God designed us to need all those vitamins and fibers—it's important to incorporate them into our diet.

Avoid fad diets. Any diet that's unbalanced to either side of the scale—either eating all fat, all fiber, or all fruit—is going to be unhealthy. Follow God's design by eating a wide variety of foods in moderation.

Try once-a-month cooking. Get together with a friend and take an entire Saturday to buy and cook meals for the next few weeks. Make healthy casseroles and sauces that you can pull out and reheat in a matter of moments. Once-a-month cooking is a great way to maximize your time in the kitchen by preparing multiple meals at once. (There is a book available that will help with the details; it's listed at the end of the chapter.)

Bottom line: A healthy diet for both you and your little ones will make a significant difference in all other aspects of your day. As you feel better about what you eat, you'll respond better to stressful situations and your children will as well. Preparing nutritious meals does take some extra effort, but it is definitely worth the investment of time and energy. Good luck!

Additional Resources

Carter, Carrie, M.D. *Mom's Health Matters*.

Larimore, Walt, M.D. *The Highly Healthy Child*.

Little, Diedre. *Fit for Eternity: Balanced Living through Better Nutrition and Spiritual Health*.

Rubin, Jordan S. *The Maker's Diet*.

Sears, William, M.D. *Family Nutrition Book*.

VanCleave, Janice. *Food and Nutrition for Every Kid*.

Wilson, Mimi, and Mary Beth Lagerborg. *Once-a-Month Cooking*.

12

Exercise

I glanced into the backseat at the stoplight. Sami's head was tilted back, and her mouth hung open. Her cheeks were rosy, and her long hair hung in wisps around her face. I wanted to take a picture, capture her beauty, but instead I just stared at her—until the light turned green and the ever-so-insensitive driver behind me honked.

The day had started with my typical list of chores. I had to vacuum, empty the dishwasher, do laundry, yada, yada, yada. But it was a beautiful day, and the blue sky and scent of spring beckoned. So I stuffed a few stray things under the couch, stuck a load in the washer, and off we went. We ended up at a small park just a few miles away. Sami ran right for the swings with me following close behind. "Push me, Mom! Push me!" I did. Then I showed her some of my own swinging talent. I pumped as hard as I could, straining for the sky, and then at the height of one jump, I let go of the chains, felt that strange flying sensation, and landed with a thump. And a jolt. And pain. Hmmmm. I'd been so much more graceful in elementary school.

But Sami was still impressed as she shouted, "Again, Mommy, do it again!" I declined as I envisioned another jump, a worse fall, and explaining it all to the doctor in the emergency room.

Yeah. I could already imagine his smirk.

So instead, I stayed on the ground. I pushed my girl, then moments later, raced her up the hill to the top of a long slide. Down we went, ran back up. Down we went again, walked back up. Down we went the third time and had to pause to catch our breath as we wondered how the hill had suddenly gotten so much bigger.

The whole afternoon was like that. Swings, slides, the little tube things that you can crawl through, the seesaw (had to be careful on that one), the monkey bars—she couldn't make it all the way across those, so I carried her halfway. By the time two hours had passed, we'd done it all.

And we were both tuckered out.

So when we stopped at that stoplight, I couldn't help but admire my sleeping girl. We'd just spent such sweet time together; we'd worked our bodies and giggled lots.

Later on, after dinner, I gave Sami her bath and tucked her into bed. She slept soundly that night—as did I. I knew it was the exercise that helped. It was so good for both of us to get out and run a bit.

It's good for all of us to get some exercise. No matter what it looks like, if we can get our hearts pumping, get our kids moving, there's nothing but benefit. So let's look at some reasons for getting exercise and then some practical ways to make it happen as a single mom of a preschooler.

Exercise Matters

Activity promotes sweet sleep. I'm sure you've experienced this too. After a day of activity out in the sun, swimming at the pool, or playing at the park, your child falls fast asleep. There's nothing like activity to burn up some of their energy. And such sweet sleep is a gift. Not only for them but also for us.

Exercise builds healthy habits. Ellie started taking Josiah for walks when he was still in his stroller. Every day she'd get up early and walk through the neighborhood to enjoy the sunshine and prepare her mind for work. By the time Josiah was a little older, he liked to ride his bike beside her—training wheels and all. He'd keep up with her or pull ahead just enough to inspect a bug, stick, or some other treasure tucked into the dirt. By the time Josiah was a teenager, he was on the track team, going out and running every day; he'd developed a lifestyle of health. When he transitioned to running on his own, it was the most natural thing in the world. It's what he'd always known.

It's good to get your kids out and doing things when they're young. Most won't end up on the track team, but they might try out for basketball, go for swimming, or at least remain active in some way.

The hard thing about being a single mom is that it's often tempting to let our kids spend too much time in front of the TV. We're tired, we've had a full week, and it's hard to get ourselves moving, much less our kids. But little outings make a difference in building healthy habits. You don't have to climb a mountain or swim laps in an Olympic-sized pool, but being active several times a week will set your kids up to continue that practice into adulthood.

Exercise builds relationship. It's amazing. You'll go out with the intent to get some exercise, play in the park, be outdoors for a hike . . . and along the way you'll run smack into relationship. That's the beautiful thing about this particular topic. Most of the exercise your child will get will be in your company, doing some of the things talked about below. In the midst of those moments, you'll get to savor the outdoors together, laugh out loud, and thoroughly enjoy the relationship. (Most times, anyway—we've gone on a few excursions where we've grumped at each other—but you get my drift. Being together, out and about, is usually a good thing!)

Here are just a few practical suggestions, ways to get exercise with your kids. Think about what might work for you and plan one of them for the coming week. Why not? You have to start somewhere. I'll tell you what; I'll do the same. Even though Sami is thirteen, we can use the exercise as well (maybe even more). I'll pick one of these too. So here we go.

- *Mini-adventure hikes.* This one's fun. Make up an adventure. Maybe someone stole the best leaf of fall and you have to go track it down. Yes, that'd be good. Pretend it's been rumored that the grand leaf thief may have dropped the leaf on his way through the local park. See if you can spot footprints, broken twigs, and perhaps even the stolen leaf along the way. Have fun with it. Or make a map. It doesn't even have to be accurate. You could draw a few squiggly lines on a piece of paper and then try to follow it by walking in squiggly lines through the park. Your little one will giggle! Or do no preparation. Go take a walk. Find cool stuff along the way. Enjoy each other. Enjoy the beauty. Have fun.

- *Swimming*. Swimming is great exercise and your child will love it. There's something about playing in the pool with mom, trying to dunk her, laughing out loud. Most towns have a community center with an indoor pool for the winter months and something outside for the summer months as well.

- *Kid aerobics*. Have you seen those videos where little kids jump around to music? They're lots of fun for some kids. My daughter didn't go for them. (Okay, I confess, I didn't either. Rather than following along and getting into it, I usually ended up sitting on the couch, watching.) But they might work for you and your family—especially if you're more focused than I am.

- *Biking*. It's just fun. If you have an area to bike in, go for it.

- *Dances/plays/dramas*. These are perfect for those days when you're not really up to a lot of physical activity yourself. Give your child the idea for a play; make it full of action with dancing monkeys (or whatever works for you). Let your kids put their imaginations to work and then let them know when the show will start. Or you can pick a song and let them make up a dance. Or if they're the more dramatic type, let them star in their own drama, complete with bad guys, good guys, and a good chase. Add to the fun by setting up a few chairs and a few stuffed animals (or siblings) to watch the production. Serve little healthy snacks.

There are so many ways to keep your kids exercising. And if you're not one to follow a list or get too profound about it, send them outside and tell them to create their own fun, making sure they're in a safe area. That's what my mom did, and aside from a few skirmishes with neighbors and the occasional eating of bugs, it worked pretty well.

Your Turn

I can almost hear you groan from here. *Exercise for me? With everything else going on, you're going to talk to me about exercise?* Don't worry, friend, I promise to be gentle. I understand that this topic may not be very high on your priority list. I know it wasn't for me. Begin by thinking in terms of lifestyle. If you're in retail or the restaurant business, if you're on your feet all day, skip this section and go to the next chapter. You probably have sore feet even as you're reading this, and you don't need to hear me drone on about exercise. But for others of you who have a sedentary lifestyle, take a look at a few of these reasons (inspirations) for getting out there and getting your heart pumping.

Exercise improves focus and attitude. Exercise keeps me on track. I don't know what it is, but when I actually take the time to get my heart pumping a few times a week, it makes a difference in my perspective. I suppose it could be a vanity thing—I feel better when I've worked out and I'm looking better, but I don't think that's totally it. My brain seems to work better when I get some exercise. Since I'm at my computer most of the day, I need to take a little time during the day to work out. Then I'm better able to focus on my work, and I seem to have a better attitude (so say my cubicle mates anyway).

Exercise helps you sleep better. You sleep better if you get some exercise during the day. I haven't really noticed, because this is one area I've never really struggled with. I'm exhausted by the time I fall into bed. It's a rare night (usually one where I'm worrying needlessly or too hot or too cold) when I don't get to sleep. But in talking with my fellow single moms, exercise helps. The only caution is exercising at night. Getting those endorphins going right before bed might leave you awake for a while, so exercise earlier in the day.

Exercise promotes good health. This is probably the greatest benefit of exercise. Getting sick as a single mom of a preschooler is absolutely the worst. Your child can't take care of you, you can't take care of yourself, and bottom line? Life must go on. Being sick isn't a viable option. Taking the time to exercise will help you fight off most illnesses.

What You Can Do

What are some ways to squeeze a workout into your busy day? Maybe some of these ideas will help.

Remember the kids. Your best workout (relationally, physically, emotionally) will be the one you can get in with your children—playing, running, biking, hiking. If you can work that in twice during the week and once on the weekend, you'll be on your way—and so will your kids.

Try lunch hour workouts. This has been great for me. I work out over my lunch hour and then grab a bite to eat at my desk. For me, it's been a great option. If you can't walk around the outside of your workplace, find a local gym (check on single-parent family discounts), or walk the halls; all of those will work. A group of women at my office power-walk through the building. I ran into a group of them rounding a corner once. It wasn't pretty. So if you do it, be careful coming around corners.

Try morning workouts. This definitely depends on your wiring. Are you a morning person? I love getting up in the early morning quiet. It's my time. I spend some time reading the Bible and journaling. I used to work out during this time too—me and my kickboxing video, 6:00 a.m. I know I must have been a sight to see: SpongeBob boxers, sweatshirt, hair every direction, karate-kicking my basement walls. But hey, I figure if my neighbors went through all the trouble of looking in my windows, they deserved the shocking sight of me prancing around with SpongeBob.

Bottom line: Exercise is important for you and your kids. You don't have to exercise every day, but see if you can get in twenty minutes a couple of times a week. You'll feel better. Your heart will be happy. The sun will shine. Riches will come pouring from the sky. Okay, maybe not. Do trust me on this though. At the very least, you *will* feel better.

Oh, and remember: it's always a good idea to check with a physician before starting a new program. That will keep you out of harm's way.

Additional Resources

McGinty, Alice B. *Staying Healthy: Let's Exercise*.
Miller, Helen. *Nutrition and Fitness: 50 Lessons and Exercises*.
Omartian, Stormie. *Exercise for Life* video.
Rabe, Tish. *Oh, the Things You Can Do That Are Good for You!*

Let's Get Practical

13

Discipline

Everybody knew his name. William James Jameson (changed for the purposes of the book). We all knew it because we heard it screeched across the fellowship hall every Sunday. "William James Jameson, get over here RIGHT NOW!" I don't think Billy liked being called by his full name because he never responded. Instead, he ducked behind anything close and giggled as his mom, Janet, grew more and more agitated. When she finally came near, he dashed between legs, under tables, and around various breakables as he tried to get away from her.

It drove us all crazy.

When I was a teenager, I knew Billy pretty well. I'd babysat him a number of times, and he had the same problem at home. He never listened.

"Oh, he means well," his mom told me on one occasion. "He just can't sit still." And then she said the same thing she said to me every time Billy misbehaved: "Don't be too hard on him. He misses his dad. We divorced several years ago; have I told you that?"

Unfortunately, Janet's plan backfired. In her desire not to make things worse, she didn't address any of Billy's bad behavior. He got away with anything and everything, and as he grew older, he assumed the world was there to cater to his needs—that he could still do anything and everything without dealing with consequences. His cute little tantrums as a preschooler turned into a violent temper when he was a teenager. Being disrespectful to people, choosing not to work, expecting others to take care of him . . . all those behaviors started when, as a child, he was allowed to dishonor his mom, ignore his chores, and demand help for things he could do on his own. Even now, Billy struggles with taking any responsibility for his actions. He's a spoiled little boy in a grown-up body. His mom didn't give him a gift by letting him get away with stuff; she actually sabotaged his future.

Discipline Matters

Most of us, as we read about Billy, can understand the value of discipline. We can step back and objectively say that Janet didn't help Billy by letting him get away with stuff. But for some of us, even knowing that doesn't make much of a difference. When it comes to our own kids, we see things differently. We know their stories. We know their hearts and their hurts and their longings, so we may be tempted to avoid discipline for any number of reasons. Whatever our situation, sometimes we just need a reminder about the value of standing firm.

Standing firm sets your child up well. Eventually, your little one is going to go out into the world, go to school, rent an apartment, do laundry, and pay bills. If you don't help corral their wild impulses as children, they will have a difficult time doing life well. They won't understand things like delayed gratification—that if they want a car, they'll need to work hard and save. Or if they want to be healthy, they'll have to eat well and exercise. On the flip side, if we train them to clean their rooms, respect other people, work hard, and eat their veggies, they'll be prepared and equipped when they go beyond our doorstep.

Standing firm keeps your child safe. I compare this to our relationship with God. I used to get angry with God about the rules he imposed. It felt as if Christianity was all about the "don'ts," and honestly, it didn't seem like a whole lot of fun. So I went my own way and had all the fun I could possibly pursue. And I discovered something. Going my own way wasn't that fun after all. Smoking became an addiction, drinking made me do things I normally wouldn't do, and violating God's design for purity left me with a boatload of heartache. Then I discovered something else. As I got to know God's heart and his character, I realized that his rules weren't meant to rob me of fun, they were meant to keep me safe. Now I cling to those rules. They protect me.

It's the same thing with our kids. They may not like the rules we set in place, and they may think we're just robbing them of fun, but honestly, we're keeping them safe. We want them to hold our hand so they won't dash into the street. We want them to eat their veggies so they can avoid illness and grow strong. We want them to go to bed on time so they can be well rested and learn throughout the day. And our kids won't be much different from us. They may not like the rules at first, but when they look back on it, when they're older and know the joy of a disciplined life, they will thank us. They will understand that our discipline was all about their safety.

Standing firm makes life easier. I have been known to be a pushover. I don't know why I keep confessing these things to you, but it's true. Sami has looked at me with those big green eyes and that toothy grin, and I've forgotten what I could possibly be angry about. Pouring sugar on the floor isn't that big a deal, is it? So she forgot to brush her teeth, they'll all fall out eventually, won't they? I often caved and bought into her "But I forgot!" or "I didn't mean to . . ." or "The cat made me do it!" Problems came with my inconsistency though. Sami learned that on some occasions I didn't follow through on consequences. Which, in her mind, gave her the edge. If she had a chance, why not push? Why not whine? Why not add in a little tantrum in hopes that I might change my mind? And she's no fool—if I gave in once before, there's a good chance that I might give in again.

Consistent discipline takes away that edge. If your child knows that you will follow through on whatever consequences you've set in place, he or she won't even bother to fight it. Sami, now thirteen, understands this. I'm a different woman these days. In fact, yesterday she forgot to make her bed. On days when she forgets to make her bed, she can't go anywhere that night. She had plans last night, and they were canceled because of her choice. She didn't even question whether I would follow through. She wasn't very happy about it and she even gave me the silent treatment for a little while, but she didn't fight it.

I've learned my lesson. Following through with consistent discipline makes life much easier.

What about you? Are you consistent in your discipline? As I was talking with other moms, I found there were three factors that contribute to their wavering on discipline. See if any of them sound familiar to you.

1. "I'm tired." Sometimes I just didn't care. I was tired; I'd had a long day. If Sami wanted to eat Play-Doh or dress the dog in my panty hose, she could go for it. I just didn't have it in me to address it. There were different occasions when I pretended not to notice stuff—like the peas she slid under the edge of her plate or the chocolate chip cookie she swiped and hid under her shirt (leaving little brown spots all over her belly). In those moments the discipline would take more energy than I had in me. I chose to ignore it.

While this isn't a huge thing on some occasions, if we're consistently tired and we consistently ignore bad behavior, we're not setting our children up well. Do what it takes to avoid ignoring behavior because of exhaustion, whether that means getting to bed earlier or pushing through to address issues even when you're tired.

2. "He's been through enough." Janet (the woman whose story kicked off this chapter) couldn't bear to discipline her son because she felt bad for him. She knew he'd been through some tough things, and she felt that disciplining would only add to his sadness. The truth is the exact opposite. If a child has been through a hard time, discipline communicates safety, love, consistency, and hope. If other things have fallen apart in their lives, they need to know and understand what is expected at home. If you offer loving and consistent discipline, they will feel better equipped to handle life when it does get

messy. Of course, your child won't see this and may put up a fuss. Not one of us likes to be told what to do, even if it is in our best interest. Your child will especially have a hard time if you haven't been consistent in the past. But ultimately, he or she will get over it—and will thrive in a disciplined environment.

My daughter came to me the other day and shared about a friend of hers. "Her mom doesn't care what she does. Isn't that sad? She never gets in trouble, never gets asked about stuff . . . I'm glad you're not like that." What I heard my daughter saying is that as much as she gripes and groans about rules and restrictions, she knows they communicate love. And the sad thing is, I know her friend's mom. She's a kind woman, but she's afraid to discipline her children because she feels "they've already been through enough."

3. "I don't want him to hate me!" John has tried to play his mom, Denise. He spends the weekend with his dad with minimal rules, then comes home and lays a guilt trip on his mom. "Dad lets me have all the dessert I want and he doesn't care what I watch. Come on, you're being mean!" When her five-year-old first spoke those words, hands on his hips, Denise's heart sank. She was tempted to change her rules to adapt to his father's, but after some conversation with friends, she thought better of it. But it was tempting. Why? Because she wanted to be liked—whether there is another parent involved or not, some of us struggle with discipline because we don't want our children to hate us. We think that setting boundaries will make them angry and jeopardize the relationship. And if we've already been through loss, the fear of further loss can leave us weak and ineffective in our parenting.

Again, the truth: if we are firm with our kids, if we discipline them, they will love us. In fact, they will love us all the more because, intuitively, they long for us to be the parent we're supposed to be—to protect them with rules and guidelines designed for their safety. Even if we run into resistance initially, children love and respect a grown-up who takes their role and their authority seriously.

What You Can Do

So we know the value of discipline, and we understand the reasons we might waver, but what does discipline look like? How can we discipline our kids in a way that will best equip them for the future?

Be firm and follow through. There is a balance that comes with being firm. We want to be serious but not go overboard and raise our voice or lose our temper. Commit to yourself that you won't raise your voice but you will stick to your guns. If your children willfully defy you, let them experience the consequence. For Sami, my correcting her was enough for her to fall apart; she hated when I would get even a little angry. Talking to her often did the trick. Other kids respond best to a time-out or loss of privileges. Remember though, don't punish out of emotion. Always make sure you follow through calmly.

Be consistent. If you correct a behavior on Monday, make sure you correct the same behavior on Wednesday. Otherwise you'll run into the problem I described earlier: a kid who's figured out that with just a little pushing, she can get her way.

Pick your battles. Make sure your discipline is age appropriate. Don't punish your four-year-old for not acting like a ten-year-old. I was at the grocery store the other day when I saw a mom swat a young child for singing. Singing! I've seen other parents get after their kids for giggling, playing, or just being kids. Kids are supposed to be childish—they knock things over, they play when they should sit still, they like coloring outside the lines. Discipline your children for willful defiance, when they're jeopardizing their safety, or when they are disrespectful. Let the other things go—kids need to be kids.

Separate your love from the punishment. I haven't always done this well, but I'm learning. When Sami makes a lousy choice, I try to grieve with her. "Wow, what a bummer," I've said. "Now you won't be able to spend the night with your friends." I let her experience the consequence, but I try to avoid letting her feel as if she is bad. We've all heard it, the mom who demeans her child because of something he or she did. Don't ever call your child names or withdraw love because of their behavior. Just let them experience whatever the consequence might be and make sure they know that your love remains intact, solid, and unchangeable.

Read books. There are lots of good resources available on this topic. Contact a Christian counselor you trust or check with another trusted professional and see what books they would recommend. I have some listed at the end of the chapter, but if you'd like to try something different, go for it. The more educated you are about discipline, about your child's wiring, the better you'll be able to set specific, practical, and healthy guidelines in your home.

Bottom line: Remember, your kids need you to be their mom. They need you to protect them, guide them, and train them for the future. Don't be afraid to step into that role and all that it entails. Be firm, consistent, and choose your battles wisely. It will make a difference.

Additional Resources

Buchanan, Margaret. *Parenting with Purpose.*

Dobson, James. *The New Dare to Discipline.*

McPherson, Miles. *Parenting the Wild Child.*

Richmond, Gary. *Successful Single Parenting.*

Townsend, John, and Henry Cloud. *Raising Great Kids.*

Turansky, Scott, and Joanne Miller. *Good and Angry: Exchanging Frustration for Character . . . in You and Your Kids!*

14

Responsibilities

Four-year-old Andrew liked to be busy. Busy, busy, busy. From the moment he stepped in the door from preschool to the moment his tired mom, Lina, put him to bed, he was constantly in motion—pulling toys from shelves, playing with Matchbox cars, building sand castles in the sandbox. Lina's two older children were more low key. But Andrew—that boy wore her out.

One Friday afternoon Lina went to the grocery store, leaving the older kids in charge. Upon her return, she started unloading the groceries and then paused. Like a deer unsettled by the sounds in a forest, she froze, eyes wide as she listened. Nothing. She didn't hear a thing, and with Andrew around, that was a near impossibility. Heart pounding, she hurried into the living room. No one. She ran upstairs. The two older kids were in their shared room, working on homework.

"Where's Andrew?" she cried, already imagining the worst.

"Chill, Mom," said her oldest. "He's cleaning the bathroom."

"He's what?"

"We told him we'd give him a quarter if he would just stop talking and clean the bathroom."

Lina moved down the hallway and peeked her head around the bathroom door. There he was, using a washcloth on the bathroom floor. Andrew was concentrating on a spot that Lina already knew wasn't going anywhere. But he was focused, and unbelievably, he was quiet. Lina looked around the rest of the bathroom. He'd pushed the toiletries back on the counter and wiped it down. He'd missed a few spots, but it was obvious he tried. The toilet lid was closed. There were even a few streaks on the mirror. Lina realized he must have climbed up on the counter to take a few swipes. She decided not to interrupt him. She backed away and went downstairs to her groceries.

Imagine that. Her son, doing housework! She glanced out the window. Nope, no flying pigs—but truly, a stranger day she hadn't known.

Lina smiled. She may have stumbled on to something. She'd always given the older kids chores to complete, but it hadn't occurred to her to ask Andrew to pitch in. She thought he was too young, that he should be able to play. She didn't realize that he might actually like doing chores.

Responsibility Matters

Kids need responsibility. Like Lina discovered, when given the opportunity, they like to be a part of things.

Granted, they may not complete a certain task well, but they definitely like to help. Some folks think kids shouldn't have to work. "They're kids," they say. "They deserve to play . . . to be kids." While that's true, it's equally valuable for children to feel that they have an important role in the family.

Other parents don't like to push their children because the kids have been through a difficult time. Perhaps they've just come through a divorce situation or they've lost a parent to death; the remaining parent may not want to ask "too much" of the children, thinking it won't be good for them. The exact opposite is actually true.

Let's take a look at some of the reasons responsibility is a plus in the life of a child.

Responsibility builds self-esteem. Sami, at five years old, was certain that the yard looked a thousand times better. "You did a pretty good job with the lawn mower, Mommy," she said, "but I think it looks much better now." She stood with her hands on her hips, surveying the vast expanse of our backyard. All thirty square feet of it looked mighty fine. "You probably couldn't get all the little pieces," she said, glancing in my direction, looking me up and down. "You're too big."

I nodded, very serious. "You're right, Sami; if you hadn't picked up all those broken leaves and twigs, I never would have seen them."

"Yeah," she said, sighing. "Good thing you have me."

I almost laughed out loud, but instead, I choked it down and coughed. She couldn't have been any cuter. "Yeah, good thing."

We went inside and I went to the refrigerator. "Want something to drink?"

She looked like a mini-me as she wiped her brow. "Yes. I'm thirsty. Some lemonade, please."

As she sat at the kitchen table, I couldn't help but marvel at how grown-up she seemed. It was as if the simple act of helping me, of feeling needed, caused her to sit up straighter and act more mature. She was proud, thrilled that she could help out with something I "couldn't" do by myself.

It's important for us to involve our kids in simple tasks around the house. As they contribute, and as we recognize them, they feel better about their abilities. They'll know they are needed, and when they approach larger tasks in the future (homework, sports, etc.), they'll have the confidence to complete them. Even if it's just helping out in the yard, around the kitchen, or in their room, give your kids the chance to contribute and then compliment them for their effort.

One caution: be careful not to come right behind them and redo what they've just done. I've been busted doing this a few times. Sami helped with something, and because she was little, it didn't quite come out the way I would have done it. So without even thinking, I'd follow right behind, cleaning the same spot. More than once I've caught Sami looking at me with that wounded look. "Didn't I do a good job, Mom?" I'd have to scramble, apologize, and remind her that I'm old and forgetful and goofy sometimes—which not too surprisingly, she bought.

Responsibility builds a sense of family. All for one and one for all! There's nothing like the feeling of belonging to something bigger than ourselves whether it's a group of friends, a sports team, or a family. We need to belong. And taking ownership for the overall well-being of that group increases those feelings. Kids need to know that what they do matters to the whole family. If your child helps to set the table, remind him or her about the value of the task: "Good job, Brian. Helping to set the table is important. Now we can all sit together and hear about each other's day. Well done!" Tie the task to the concept of family and watch how your child swells with pride.

Responsibility builds an awareness beyond "me." Every child feels like the world does (or should) revolve around him or her. Since they were infants, their smallest accomplishments were celebrated with trumpets and noisemakers ("Wahoo! The first step!" "Yippeee! What an adorable burp!"). Then, if they sing a tune, if they build something big, if they jump up and down especially well, we're called to "Watch me! Watch me!" so the celebration will continue. While this is natural to every child, helping around the house helps our kids to think beyond themselves. Scrubbing the toilet keeps them humbled a bit; working to set the table reminds them of a world beyond their own and that there are other folks in that world. Serving the family as a whole is a good reminder that as much as we celebrate who they are, serving others is what it's all about.

Responsibility builds a good work ethic. We've all run into the kid, the adult, the employee, or even the employer, who thinks work is beneath them. They dilly when they should be preparing for the day and dally when they should be working. There's nothing more irritating. One of my good friends (whom I promised to keep anonymous) is extremely frustrated with her teenager. Her teen won't clean her room (or if she does, it's halfway); she puts in minimal effort on her schoolwork and will cut every corner she possibly can. Granted, we can't always prevent these things in our kids, but in my friend's situation, she knew she'd let her daughter slide. "I didn't have her do anything when she was little, and now she hates any kind of infringement on her time," my friend says. "She feels 'above' helping out in our home. Now I'll have to be extra hard on her until she gets it. I wish I'd trained her when she was little and didn't roll her eyes so much."

It's good to be proactive by giving our kids the opportunity to work hard and then feel good about that work. When your child finishes a task, praise him for his effort and then give him feedback. If the job was done halfway, have him do it over. Granted, the job may not be perfect. But you know your child; you know when he is slacking. If the work is good for his age level, be positive. If it's less than you know he is capable of, don't be afraid to send him back to the task. You're not being mean; you're just teaching your child how to do his best. That's a good thing! As children learn to work hard, the payoff will last for the rest of their lives. It's worth it to instill in them a good work ethic.

What You Can Do

Okay, so you're on board (if you weren't already). You think it would be good for your child to contribute to your home. But now you're wondering what types of tasks would be best suited for a preschooler. I know some of this will seem basic, but other ideas may be new to you. Read on and go with what will work for your family.

Assign daily chores. Make a chart of daily chores for each child. At the end of the day, go through those chores and mark off the ones completed well. Preschoolers can make their bed, help set the table, and pick up dirty clothes. On Saturdays, have a special chore chart. In the morning, assign each child a few tasks and then look them over. They can help carry clothes from the laundry room back to their room and help put them away. They can also help sweep the floor or clean up their rooms. By working together, the chores will get done that much more quickly—then take the rest of the day on Saturday to do something fun as a family. Also, take breaks and make your cleaning time fun. Sami and I used to turn the music up and dance through our chores. The neighbors didn't like us much, but my daughter still enjoys turning on some good music and working on her room. For us, music made it more fun.

Okay, pause. I'm feeling bad. I again have to confess something. While charts can be good, I've never used them. I think I made one once, put it up on the bathroom mirror, and marked it up one Saturday. It stayed up for three months until it eventually curled and fell to the ground—to be tossed on the following chore day. So do this: if a chart works for you, go for it. If it doesn't, still have your child complete chores, just give hugs instead of stars or check marks.

Know your child's wiring. You'll always have daily chores that every child should get done. But before you assign any extra chores or tasks, it's helpful to understand your child's wiring. Maybe he or she has a real interest in putting things together or organizing. For that child, organizing a drawer would be a little slice of heaven. For your wild one though, organizing a drawer will be the most difficult task ever, whereas picking up sticks (and seeing how many he can collect) or dust-bunny hunting (the creative way to get them dusting) would be much more appealing. Give tasks where you know they'll experience success. That will only build their interest, work ethic, and sense of accomplishment.

Consider buying a pet. In addition to chores and charts, tasks that are mundane, and tasks that will nurture your children's gifts, you can consider getting your child a pet. Depending on your child's maturity level, the pet could be a snail (with minimal needs) or a kitten (with greater needs). Pets are wonderful for training our kids to take responsibility. If you're concerned about a pet's welfare at the hands of your child, consider one of the sturdier options (snails, crabs, goldfish). Any of those, and I mean this in the nicest possible way, can be easily flushed and replaced.

If your child seems able to handle the responsibility, consider something that needs more attention (dog, cat). Pets offer an amazing opportunity for children to really mature in thinking beyond themselves. Sami has always had some kind of pet in her life. We've had everything from fish and kittens to snakes and dogs. Reeses, our dog now, has been part of our family for six or seven years. He's been Sami's companion, wrestling partner, and friend. Taking care of him has added to our world. He's part of the family.

Even if it's just a little goldfish your children will need to feed every day, consider a pet as a way to help them grow in their willingness to take responsibility.

Bottom line: Kids need to know that they have a role in the family. By giving them specific tasks to accomplish, you bolster their self-esteem, get them thinking beyond themselves, and help them to build a strong work ethic that will serve to equip them in the future. Don't be afraid to take steps and train your child in the value of responsibility. And it's never too early to start!

Additional Resources

Clarkson, Sally. *The Mission of Motherhood*.
Menashe, Joyce. *I Love Chores* (Coffeehouse Publishers).
Steward, Jennifer. *Choreganizers*.
Together Teamwork, Jay Jay the Jet Plane, Video #9.

15

Finances

I never liked thinking about money. And honestly, I didn't much see the point. Any money that came in went right back out again. And why budget when there was nothing to budget? The fact is, I'd learned how to live without my basic wants, and for the most part my bills were paid on a monthly basis. I did pretty well adjusting to my limited income, three fuzzy channels on the TV, and ramen noodle dinners. I'd even come to terms with the fact that cell phones were for the rich and famous, of which I was neither—and that a night out meant showing up at my brother's doorstep for dinner and (if I was lucky) dessert.

While I did well adapting to those things, I hated one particular aspect of being poor. Welfare. You may think *hate* is a strong word, but that was the feeling I had. I was grateful there was a resource available to me, but I didn't like the way I felt standing in line, I didn't like how some folks treated me, and most of all I didn't like standing in the grocery store, food stamps in hand. I always felt that those standing behind me evaluated what I bought and, if I had any brand-name items, that they judged me for wasting their money. Oh, I was probably projecting some of my own shame, but no matter. The feeling itself was enough of a motivator for me to do anything I could to change my situation.

What moved me forward was a message I heard at my brother's church. Folks there were encouraged to set up a budget, no matter what their income. "By keeping track of where the money goes," one gentleman said, "you'll find you're spending money on things you didn't even realize you were spending it on. And once you start documenting it and setting up a monthly plan, you can begin to slowly build your savings and pay off any debt you have."

That was music to my ears. For some reason, I'd ended up with all the debt in the divorce. All the credit cards were in my name, and we'd maxed out each one of them. I wanted out of debt, and I wanted some savings. Most of all, I wanted off welfare. So they had my ear—grudgingly.

Budgeting Matters

Budgeting does matter, for each of us, no matter what our income. But maybe you're like me, and you need some added incentive to go through the effort. If so, think on these things.

Pay off debt. Debt robs us. Not only does it rob us financially of the interest we pay, but also it robs us of our emotional well-being. On too many occasions I've been irritable with Sami because the credit card bill was due. She didn't have a thing to do with it, but she paid the price (pun intended) with my attitude. Having a clean slate will definitely take a load off your emotional and financial shoulders. Budgeting will help bring that to pass.

Build emergency savings. One thing budgeting taught me was that paying myself was as important as paying off creditors. As I set a monthly plan, I made savings a bill that I paid too. Granted, it was a very small bill, but I still paid it. And it came in handy—like the time I was singing in my car, hit the curb, and needed a new tire; or when my washing machine broke; or when my dog ate a foreign object and needed the vet. Budgeting will help you set up a fund to take care of those not-so-every-day expenses.

Know where your money goes. I was surprised to discover how much money I spent on stupid stuff. I thought I wasn't spending anything—but as I kept track, I found that I spent money on fast food, coffee from the convenience store, movie rentals, and the occasional junk food spree that turned out to be more than occasional. As I realized how much cash was going out for items I'd never see again, I determined to cut back. Fries didn't constitute a necessary food item (no matter how much Sami disagreed).

Set aside fun money. Once I had a budget set up, I could put away a little money weekly for fun stuff. Instead of the quick output for fast food or a movie rental, I could save for a few weeks and actually take Sami on a little overnight or to dinner and a real movie theater (where our feet stuck to the buttery floor and everything). Wahoo!

Watch your income grow. The wonderful thing about budgeting is that once you have a budget in place, you can keep it in place as your income grows. When you become that rich and famous rock star or best-selling novelist, you'll have the skills to handle your newfound wealth. Budgeting is a great tool to have—and as your income grows with time, you'll have a good handle on your finances.

What You Can Do

So now you're inspired (or so I tell myself), but you may need some practical tools to help you. There are lots of resources out there. A great one comes from Crown Financial Ministries—you can access practical budgeting tools on their website—www.crown.org/tools. Or if you would like a human being to talk with, the same organization can direct you to a church-based counselor. Call 1-800-722-1976, and they'll help you find someone in your area. Another option is a nonprofit debt counseling service. Several organizations will work with you and your creditors to get your debt under control. If you discover one, make sure you investigate its reputation. There are several good organizations, but you always want to be careful when it comes to disclosing your finances.

Budget Tips to Decrease Outflow

Once you get your budget set up, there are some ways to minimize your spending so that you have more resources to work with. Here are a few tips.

150

Avoid credit card debt. Why pay interest? If you want something, save up the money before you purchase it. Granted, there are some occasions where that's impossible, but do what you can to pay for things in cash. I had an empty living room for the longest time. Sami and I pitched a tent in there, played, danced, had sleepovers, and so on. We were saving for a new couch, and I was determined not to go in debt. When the day finally came, I felt like a proud new mama bringing home her baby. I sat on that couch ten different ways on the first day, just to test it out. Sami giggled. It was my first big purchase—no debt. Straight cash. That was a good day.

Avoid eating out. This one's difficult. Ordering pizza or stopping for a quick burger seems almost nonnegotiable in single-parent life. But there are ways to enjoy a quick, fast-food meal without busting your budget. If you know you'll do pizza once a week, get some of the frozen ones at the grocery store. Keep an eye out for sales—it's at least $10.00 cheaper to buy a pizza there instead of getting one delivered. Or buy burger patties and cook one up when you need something fast. Yes, it goes against our nutrition chapter, but we all know how it is: sometimes life just calls for burgers and pizza. Just make sure to pick up a bag of salad and a few cans of green beans to accompany your choice.

Buy in bulk. I don't usually enjoy buying in bulk. I look at those monster boxes of toilet paper, and I can't imagine carting them out to my car or where I will store them when I get home. But truthfully, bulk is the better way to go. For items that aren't perishable, bulk buying will save you bucks.

Cut coupons. If you're good at this, go for it. If you're not good at it, give it a shot one more time. If you're like me, don't bother. I've tried several times to cut coupons and usually end up forgetting them, not liking the product, or finding that the generic brand is cheaper than the brand name with the coupon. But that's me. I have friends who say coupon cutting is the way to financial wealth and happiness. They may be right, so I would suggest giving it a shot and deciding for yourself.

Watch for sales. This will definitely help your budget. Buy spring clothes in the summer, summer in the fall, fall in the winter, and so on. Also, think about going to places like Goodwill for deals. It's well worth it. They often have brand names at amazing prices. For food and other perishables, keep an eye on the Sunday paper for sales on items you typically purchase.

Ask for deals. Always ask about single-parent family discounts. While this doesn't apply for everyday shopping, it's great for travel, hotels, retreat centers, camps, YMCA memberships, and such. Don't be afraid to check into discounts. Many places have them available for situations like ours.

Budget Tips to Increase Income

As you prepare your budget, there are also ways to maximize your income. These tips may help.

Follow up on child support. If you are divorced, make sure you are doing all you can to collect the child support your children are due. I know several single moms who don't want to deal with the frustration of alerting the courts and getting the paperwork started. Either that, or they just don't want to anger their ex-spouse. But if child support is an option, pursue it as you are able. Your child's father is responsible for contributing to the child's financial well-being. It's not only the law; it's the right thing to do. Stand firm in pursuing that.

Monopolize on hobbies and crafts. It could be that you have a talent other people will pay money to enjoy. I have several friends who supplement their income this way. Maybe you play an instrument and can offer Saturday lessons, or you like to write and can submit articles to different magazines. You might be great at woodworking, framing, or painting knickknacks—if you are, getting involved with craft shows will give you an opportunity to earn some extra cash.

Offer to house-sit, babysit, or dog-sit. Sami and I spent many a weekend at the houses of friends, neighbors, and fellow churchgoers while they traveled on vacation. This was an easy way to earn a few extra dollars, and it was actually kind of fun to get out of our own environment. The people who could afford house sitters could usually also afford cable TV, quality junk food, and functioning toilets. We took full advantage of such amenities.

I also enjoy children, and we'd add an extra few to our Saturday activities and earn some cash that way. We also tried dog-sitting. That didn't always work quite as well. We had two cats at the time, and they had issues with bringing in strange furry creatures that wanted to eat them. But something like that might work for your situation.

Have a garage sale. A garage sale is a great way to earn some cash. Just make sure you schedule several days for this endeavor. It's a huge job to organize, price, and set everything out. If you're up for the challenge, it will work. You just have to remember that when you advertise a garage sale, people will start showing up at the crack of dawn.

I have one friend who had a fanatical garage saler knock on her door at 6:00 a.m.: "Aren't you having a garage sale today?" If my friend had already had coffee, her response might have been kinder. But as it was, I think she may have said some nasty words before she slammed the door. Just be prepared for what might come.

Ask for help. There may come a time when you are absolutely at the end of your rope. You've set up a budget, you're trying to do things well, and you get blindsided by a huge expense. This is a time when it would be good to ask for help. There are organizations and people in your life who are ready to lend a helping hand. While it's never an easy thing to do, sometimes we need to swallow our pride, let someone know our need, and watch what God does. Now this doesn't work if we're counting on others as our only source of income. People who love us won't give us money if we're depending on them instead of working. But in those unique situations where we've come to the end of ourselves, it's more than okay to ask for help. Talk to a parent, sibling, or friend. Give your church a call. Let people know of your need and accept any help that comes.

Bottom line: It will definitely be worth your time to investigate the tools we talked about and set yourself up on a budget. Do what you can to reduce spending, get creative with bringing in income, and ask for help if you need it. Many churches offer help in setting up a budget as well—and usually it's free.

Additional Resources

Barnes, Emilie. *Emilie Barnes' 15-Minute House and Budget Manager.*

Burkett, Larry. *Family Budget Workbook.*

Burkett, Larry, and Brenda Armstrong. *Making Ends Meet: Budgeting Made Easy.*

Kay, Ellie. *A Woman's Guide to Family Finances.*

Sumner, Cynthia. *Dollars & Sense: A Mom's Guide to Money Matters.*

16

Exploration

Sami and I were sipping hot chocolate when the mother and daughter came into the café and sat beside us. I don't even think they noticed us, but I noticed them. They were perfectly put together. The mother was in a tennis outfit—white shorts, beautiful white top, perfect white sneakers. The little girl, just about Sami's age, was dressed in a pink tutu, pink top, and spotless pink dancing shoes. Her hair was done up in little ponytails with ribbons tied to each one that flowed exactly the same length to the tops of her shoulders. Both mom and daughter were blonde, trim, and perfect.

Sami and I, on the other hand, were a little disheveled. I was in my cutoff jean shorts and my Lone Star Steakhouse and Saloon T-shirt. I had my ball cap on and what should have been wisps coming from beneath it looked more like chunks of unmanageable hair. I'd tried to put Sami's hair into ponytails, but I was never very good at parts. So hers was also tucked up into a ball cap, strands coming out everywhere.

Already not liking this perfect pair beside us, I listened to the woman speak with her daughter.

"We'll get you to your lesson, and then I'll go play tennis. Daddy will pick you up afterwards, and don't forget, you have gymnastics tonight. Tomorrow, you'll be able to sleep in a little bit, but not too long because we'll have to get ready for your piano recital."

I glanced at the little girl. Before I saw her face, I felt envious. How I wished I had the money for those types of things! Surely Sami would be better off with lessons and recitals and gymnastic flips and twirls! What frustrating moments were these, when everything I wanted for Sami seemed so out of reach.

But then I saw the little girl's face. She was miserable. She was glowering at her mom as her mom ran through the list of weekend activities.

"I don't want to go, Mom!" she said. "I want to go to the playground with Melissa."

"You can hang out with the neighbors anytime," her mom replied. "These things are important! Besides, you were the one that said you wanted to play piano and practice gymnastics. Now, you have to stick with it. Don't be so quick to give up on everything."

The little girl hung her head. "I'm not giving up," she pouted. "I just want to play outside today. I've been practicing all week!"

I looked from the girl back to Sami. Sami was oblivious to all that was going on. She was focused solely on the whipped cream that was melting on top of her hot chocolate. With delicate swishes of her tongue, she was trying to scoop it all up before it melted into oblivion. She had whipped cream hanging off her cheek and a bit of chocolate clinging to the end of a wayward wisp of hair. She looked up at me and caught my eye. She grinned from ear to ear. "What do ya wanna do next, Mom? Wanna do our nails? I'll paint yours if you want. Will you paint mine?" She looked at her left hand and surveyed our most recent paint job of green with pink polka dots. "I think I'll do pink with green polka dots instead. Okay? Can we do that?"

I nodded and had to smile. Maybe lessons and preschool Olympic training weren't the most important things this particular morning.

I looked again at the other little girl. She was clean and cute but miserable. I looked back at Sami. She looked happy. Disheveled and half-put-together but happy. I decided maybe it wasn't my place to be envious or critical. Life in our world was just fine.

Looking back on that day, I believe there should be a healthy balance between the priorities Sami and I lived out and the priorities of the little family beside us. It is good and healthy for kids to have specific interests and opportunities to explore those interests. It's also good for kids to play in the park, be silly, and dunk their cheeks in whipped cream.

So what does it look like to achieve that balance? How can you introduce your kids to different experiences without overwhelming them? How do you pick and choose what to let them participate in, and once you figure something out, how do you pay for it? Let's take a look at some thoughts that may help as you process your options.

What You Can Do

Before you think about signing your child up for a particular class/training/lesson, it might be a good idea to think through why you want to do it. That day in the café, I wanted to walk out the door, run over to the YMCA, and sign Sami up for the next class. I didn't want her to be deprived just because she came from a single-parent family. I wanted my girl to live a life as good as anyone else's—and if that meant lessons, recitals, and a future as an Olympian, then I wanted to do everything I could to make it happen. *Yeah*, I thought to myself. *I have everything it takes to take care of my daughter. Yeah. So there.*

But later, as I thought about my brilliant plan, I was less than happy with myself. I hadn't wanted to sign Sami up for something because it would be best for her; I really wanted to sign her up so I could look like a better mom. In that instance, my motive had nothing at all to do with Sami and everything to do with the "not enough" feeling I had when the mom and daughter walked into the café.

I've known other moms who signed their kids up just for the bragging rights. You may know moms like this. The ones in the office or the grocery store or the café who talk about their children as they might talk about any prized possession. "Yes, Suzy is a gifted musician/gymnast/artist. They say she's the best in her class. She's in six different classes now, and I'm getting ready to sign her up for the next round." Moms like these make you want to cringe. You know little Suzy can't possibly enjoy spending all of her time in classes and lessons, but her mom is using Suzy to say to the world, "Look at how good a mom I am!" It's not fair. Suzy is more than a show pony.

So before you think about signing your kids up for the next thing, it's always good to think about the "why" behind it. If your child really does show strength in co-ordination or a passion for dance, then do what you can to give him or her chances to dance. If he or she is good at coloring or drawing, pave the way to get some more opportunities to practice. But take the following steps before you consider outside instruction in a particular area.

Observe your child. One of my neighbors once signed her son up for T-ball. There was only one problem; her son hated sports. He loved to draw and would have enjoyed an art lesson, but he had not a bit of interest in playing ball. But this particular mom thought he should give it a try to see if he liked it. So she signed him up; he hated it, and both of them were extremely frustrated by the end of the experience.

While we want to expose our kids to new experiences, if they show no aptitude for athletics and no interest, we probably want to stay away from football, baseball, or basketball. On the other hand, if our child loves sports—watches it on television, plays it with the neighbors, and wants to be the next big football star, we probably don't want to sign him up for pottery and drawing classes. Oh, I suppose some may disagree and say that we need to give our kids the opportunity to become "well rounded," but what about first allowing a child to know some success in an area where he or she already has strength and interest? There will be plenty of time to explore other things as they get into elementary, middle, and high school. Let them do what they enjoy doing in this season.

Open the door. Maybe you've noticed that your son has a talent in a particular hobby—let's say drawing. He loves to color. Does that mean you have to sign him up for every class around, even as a preschooler? No, it doesn't. Expanding his world could be as simple as getting an art set and giving him some more options to express his creativity. Yes, you can sign him up for a class, but you don't have to. Simply give him other opportunities to excel in what he loves. Put his paintings up on the fridge. Celebrate his first watercolor. Be enthusiastic and nurture his particular gifts. If you want to wait and sign him up for something once he's school age, that's perfectly fine.

That's the key. Notice strengths, nurture them as best as you are able, and give him the tools to practice. Despite what anyone else may say, that is good enough for this season of life.

If, however, you would like to get your child signed up for outside instruction, if he is interested and you think it would be a good step with your schedule and finances, here are some ideas to help make it happen.

Look for classes. Most communities have some type of community center or YMCA. Depending on where you live, they might offer classes. Go to that center and check things out. If possible, show up before or after a class that is already in session. See if the kids are happy; talk to the instructor and the parents of other kids. If there are no community centers or local YMCAs, check with the city. Sometimes, the city will offer different classes, and the parks and recreation department will have the details. If nothing like that is available, talk to the teachers at your child's day care or preschool. They may know of some folks who give private lessons in a particular area. Finally, check the Yellow Pages. If you go that route though, make sure you can get some references and take the time to observe some of the classes. Usually, classes are pretty short for younger kids; if that's the case, stick around and make sure you get what you pay for.

Try to cut costs. Getting our kids signed up for different things can become a huge financial burden. Depending on what it is, you can also have uniform cost, shoes, supplies, and any number of things. First, ask if there is any special discount for single-parent families. Second, ask the teacher if they know any place where you can get the supplies (extras) for a reasonable cost. The teachers themselves may have some of the items; if not, they'll know the best place to buy them. Another thought is to ask grandparents to sponsor a particular interest. Maybe they would like to help financially with lessons or classes. Some grandparents are more than willing to invest financial help in such a worthy cause.

Don't over-schedule yourself. Especially if you have other kids to take care of, guard your family time diligently. If signing your preschooler up for a class will take too much time from family, then just wait until he or she is a little older. Family should be the priority—you and your children need that the most. Or, if you can, sign the kids up for classes that take place all on the same night.

Bottom line: Remember, this season of life, though it may feel like it drags forever, will actually pass quickly. Your child will soon enter elementary school, then middle school, then high school. Savor the moments you have together. If you can nurture your children's strengths within the home so you can have the time together, go with that. If you do sign them up for classes, keep them limited to just a few times a month. Before you know it, they'll be off on their own.

As I write this, my daughter is hanging out at the mall with some of her friends. Friendships come first these days. And while I still have five or six years with her, I know that the time is coming up short. I'm amazed at how quickly it has flown; we hear this all the time, but it is so true. Enjoy your kids—there's a lifetime for classes but only a short season when you can color with them at the living room table, take them to a café, feed them hot chocolate, and watch them giggle as they dip their hair into the whipped cream. Don't miss the fun.

Additional Resources

Fortune, Don and Katie. *Discover Your Children's Gifts*.

Fuller, Cheri. *Unlocking Your Child's Learning Potential: How to Equip Kids to Succeed in School and Life*.

Gaither, Gloria. *I Am a Promise*.

Rue, Nancy. *The Fun-Finder Book: It's a God Thing*.

Part 5

Your Spiritual
Well-Being

17

Prayer

It was one of those days. The car, what was left of it, spluttered to a stop somewhere along Route 24. It was cold, and my coat was still hanging neatly in the closet at home. I'd already dropped Sami off at preschool, and I had an important meeting in about three minutes.

I stepped out of the car and tried to look strong enough to frighten away any potential creeps, yet cute enough to encourage a noble mechanic to stop on his way to work. *Please God*, I thought, *let someone stop*.

No one stopped. I refused to ponder what that said about God's hearing or my cuteness as I trudged down the road to find the nearest gas station.

It was not a good day.

Hours later, the mechanic at the station diagnosed the problem. Repairing the car would be expensive and would take a few days, he said. *Please God*, I whispered in my head, *I can't handle this. How am I going to get to work? How am I going to pay for this? Why did you let this happen?*

And so most of my prayers went. They were quick ones sent up like 9-1-1 calls in the midst of an emergency. They were grumpy ones when God didn't come through as I thought he should. And they were tired ones when I asked where he was and why he'd forgotten about me. But none of the prayers was more than a passing thought, accusation, or question—just a voice in my head to a God I hoped might hear. And honestly, I doubted he heard, or if he did, that he would intervene in my world.

But he did hear me. That incident was years ago. I made it through that day, I made it to work, I paid the mechanic—and I even realized I was capable of handling stuff I never thought I could handle on my own. So maybe the noble, handsome mechanic didn't stop and zap my car to health, but God did hear my prayer—and he answered it—despite my doubts.

Sami, on the other hand, had bigger, simpler faith than I did. She learned in Sunday school that God cared about her, about her needs, about her life. So when she prayed, it was full of expectation and anticipation. "Dear God," she would say as she clasped her hands together and knelt by her bed, "I love you. Thank you for my mommy. Thank you for my bed and my room. Thank you for my new Barney pillow. Please make the sun shine tomorrow so that the flowers will wake up—I can't wait to see them! Thank you. Amen."

Her prayers, sweet and simple, made me smile. I loved hearing her pray for me. I loved hearing her thank God for the good things in her life. I loved hearing her ask for him to be there, active, in her world. Her prayers inspired me.

Prayer Matters

Praying for our kids, letting them pray for us, praying for our own situations—all these forms of prayer have an impact on our daily lives. This may be something you already experience or something that you are just on the front end of exploring. Either way, God longs to hear from you and your kids. And this is a great time to get started.

Praying for Our Kids

One night, when Sami was about four years old, I tucked her in bed with this prayer: "Lord, please bless Sami's sleep. Thank you for creating her with such a beautiful smile, for giving her green eyes and a great laugh . . ." I peeked out from underneath my lashes to see Sami, eyes closed, grinning from ear to ear. "Thank you," I added, "for making her brave and strong too. She did so well getting that shot today . . ." I continued on, watching as I prayed. Sami's expressions changed as her eyes stayed squeezed shut—from joy to pride to laughter. She liked hearing me talk to God about her. It made her feel special, important.

I wish I'd known to pray more for her when she was a preschooler. Unfortunately, since I was in my grumpy-with-God phase, I didn't pray consistently. Yet there are so many benefits to praying out loud (and in the quiet) for our children. I pray for Sami at thirteen years old—only now it's every night. I still watch her, and she still grins from ear to ear. She loves knowing I talk to God about her. But there are other benefits to praying for our kids.

Prayer lets them hear our love. No matter what happened during daylight hours, bedtime prayer gives our

169

kids the chance to hear us thank God for them. Even if they've been disobedient or disrespectful, they discover that we're still grateful for them. Such knowledge is priceless!

Prayer teaches them whom to go to. As we pray over our children, they learn that there is a God who will listen to their own prayers. When they see prayer answered, they'll begin to believe in a God who is real and involved in their lives. Then, when they are frightened or uncertain, they can call out to that same God.

Prayer helps them believe in themselves. As we thank God for their strengths, as we set their dreams before him, our children will begin to see themselves through his eyes. And as they hear the same prayers through the years, they will begin to believe that good things will come. I've been praying for Sami's relationship with God for a long time. When I think about the one thing that might have saved me from my own poor choices, prayer is it. So I pray Sami will know a deep and abiding relationship with the One who crafted her. My hope is my prayer will sink to the core of her and become a reality. That God will raise up his hands and say, "Fine already!" with a grin on his face—and grant my request. I also pray for wonderful adventures and lots of joy to invade her world.

God answers prayer. This is the best part about prayer. You're calling out to a real God who cares deeply about your life and about the life of your child. As you pray, he will answer. He doesn't always answer the way we think he should, but he always answers. It's his nature. He's crazy about you.

I wish I'd started praying consistently when Sami was little. But I was too absorbed in the chaos around me.

So how I would love it if you had a jump start on praying for your children! Start now. Have them close their eyes and then watch their expressions. Your prayers for their future will delight them to the core—and just watching their faces will keep you grinning long into the evening.

Maybe you've never prayed out loud and it feels a little intimidating. Don't worry. It's not as hard as it might seem. You don't have to sound spiritual or throw in any fancy terms; just talk to God about your children—he wants to hear your heart. It could be as simple as this: "Dear Jesus, I love this little boy kneeling beside me. He is so very special to me. I love how he plays, giggles, and tumbles around on the floor. He's a good boy, Lord. Will you please take care of him? We both need you very much. Amen."

Teaching Your Child to Pray

There's nothing like hearing your child pray: "Dear God, please help Mommy; she's not feeling well tonight." "Dear God, I don't want to go to bed; please tell Mommy to let me stay up." "Dear God, I think my brother wants to help kids in another country; can you send him now?"

Prayers from your child will bring tears to your eyes or giggles to your heart. There's nothing sweeter, and I can only imagine that God feels the very same way. To help your child get started, try these ideas.

Kneel beside your child's bed with him or her. There's nothing that says kneeling prayers are any more effective than sitting up prayers, but little ones sometimes like the thought of kneeling. It can lend a special ritual to the prayer time. They might be a little uncertain about praying, or they might have questions about whether God even hears them. This is a good time to remind them their questions matter to God and then to answer them as best as you are able.

Encourage your child to pray for others. Ask your children if there are friends or family members they would like to pray for. Also give them the opportunity to pray for you. It helps remind them of a world beyond themselves, that Mom has needs, and they can care and pray for those needs. Not that you want to share the fact that you're fighting PMS, are angry at the world, or are financially at your wit's end, but you can ask a child to pray that Mom's smile will stay steady and that God would look out for your family. Kids like praying for those things.

Your Turn

When big things have happened in my life, I've been inclined to find my strength in chocolate. I've looked for hope in cigarettes, joy in relationships, and love in a large plate of nachos smothered in cheese. As appealing as those hiding places sounded at the time, not one of them ever really worked. I enjoyed the initial sensation, but I always felt bad about overdoing it for the wrong reasons. Which made me want to seek out another hiding place—maybe one heaping with whipped cream and nuts.

Yet whenever I take the time to pray, it has changed my attitude. I'm not sure why it takes me so long to go to God, but for whatever reason, I was one of those who went to everything else first. I'm still learning, and thankfully, he's still teaching. But prayer works. And there are a few reasons for this.

God answers prayer. I know we've said this once already. And it seems like a logical enough thing to say, but how many of us really believe it? God answers prayer. He hears our cry. He wants to have a relationship with us—open communication and connection. He is deeply invested in our lives and loves it when we come to him. While we may not always get the answer we expect, we always get the answer that is best for us.

Prayer lets us unload. My prayers used to be cleaned up and dressy. I never really went to the heart of the matter; I just thought my prayers had to sound good. Until a friend told me something different. She reminded me that God wants me to be real. He's not surprised by what I'm saying anyway, so why not be real? So I was. I've gone to God with my tears, my laughter, my joy, my fears. I've asked the hard questions and the easy ones. I've been angry and afraid. And somehow, once all of my stuff was spilled out, he met me. It wasn't always something definitive, but sometimes it would be (a call from a friend, a hug, a note in the mail). What was most amazing was the peace. I'd be completely spent, and somehow, I'd feel better. Far better than I would have felt diving into ice cream or nachos.

Prayer helps us see God. If you're anything like me, single parenthood has caused life to blur in all the wrong places. In the past, it was hard for me to think about God when I could barely keep my eyes open. Yet, when I've taken the time to pray over the years (in some seasons more than others), I've seen God better. I've seen him in the love of a friend, I've seen him through answered prayer, I've seen him as he has faithfully provided for Sami and me. God always shows up and engages in my world. But when I pray, I have the privilege of seeing it happen. I'm more in tune with what he does in response to my cries.

You could already be connected to God in prayer. Keep going; keep drawing close to him so he can meet you in this season. But if you are on the front end of praying and you're not sure how to go about it—or if you've been taught to pray in a way that feels stiff and forced, here are some tools that might help.

Write it down. I can really get going when I write down my prayers. I stay focused, I'm more real, and I tend to share my heart more. Sometimes I get distracted if I try to pray in the morning or evening. I'm usually not awake enough, and writing things down keeps me from losing my train of thought.

Be real. Whether on your knees or writing it down, be real. Talk to God from the depth of your heart. If you're angry, tell him. If you're sad, let him know. If you're scared, ask him to be there for you. Whatever you are feeling, it's okay. He wants to hear your heart, because then, as you're real with him, he can answer the real concerns of your heart.

Pray Scripture. Sometimes I don't even know what to pray. But I've gone to God's Word and prayed a certain Scripture passage over my girl or myself. When I don't have the words, I find out that God does.

Bottom line: No matter where you are on your faith journey, even if you're not sure you believe in God at all, prayer helps. I can remember when I was investigating faith, I asked God to show me who he was. "I don't love you," I told him. "I don't even know if I believe in you. But I want to believe. Will you show me how?"

God delights in answering prayers like that.

Prayer helps our children because they get to hear us pray about a good future for them. We have nothing to lose and everything to gain by praying for our kids so that they can hear us. Prayer also helps our children as they learn to pray for themselves. Prayer gives them an outlet when they're scared; it gives them a place to go and a way to love others. And for you, prayer gives you a place to go with your hurts, your fears, and your joy. It gives you the chance to unload, to connect, and to be real. Best of all, it gives you access to the One who can make a real difference in your world.

Additional Resources

Books

Barber, Karen. *Surprised by Prayer: The Wonderful Ways God Answers.*
Fuller, Cheri. *When Mothers Pray.*
Graham, Franklin. *Kids Praying for Kids: 12 Month Journal.*
Jones, Sally Lloyd. *I Can Talk to God!*
Taylor, Jeannie St. John. *How to Be a Praying Mom.*

Website

Visit www.beliefnet.com; plug in "prayer"

18

Grace

It was the cold that did it. I was getting things done, following my routine, when I was sideswiped by sniffles. It started with a tickle in the back of my throat, followed by a cough and then a fever. I was miserable. It was Saturday morning and I had a to-do list as long as my arm, but I couldn't seem to get motivated to get out of bed. Three-year-old Sami came into my bedroom hair tousled, looking cute as could be in a long T-shirt. She climbed up beside me. "Mommy," she said, as she tucked in close, "you're warm!"

I was. Toasty warm and feverish. "Don't get too close, honey," I told her. "Mommy's sick."

Sami sat up and looked at me with worry. "You're sick, Mom?" Mimicking me, she placed her hand on my forehead. "Hmmmm," she said. "You ARE warm. Don't worry, I'll take care of you."

With that she jumped off the bed and made her way to the kitchen. I could hear things clanging together as she rummaged through the lower cupboards. A chair scraped across the floor, and I knew she was climbing to reach the glasses. I almost called out a warning but didn't have the energy. Minutes later, she came in with a big glass of orange juice. She was concentrating as she walked slowly across the bedroom. Orange juice licked at the edge of the glass but managed not to spill over. I reached over and took it from her.

"Drink it all up, Mommy. Orange juice is good for you."

I took a big gulp. It did taste good.

"Thank you, honey."

She grinned.

It would be wonderful if the story ended there. We could close out the scene with soft music and warm fuzzies, fading out on yet another Hallmark moment. But you know me by now, and unfortunately, that was the best part of the day—it all went downhill from there. I got sicker as the morning wore on, and Sami lost interest in taking care of me—Barney was on. Later in the day, I managed to make my way to the kitchen to find bowls and pans scattered everywhere. The living room was littered with coloring books and pencils, and the TV was blaring. There wasn't a warm fuzzy to be found as I surveyed the mess and thought of the hours I'd put in cleaning the day before. By late afternoon, Sami started to feel sick too; we were both getting grumpy, and our little duplex was getting smaller and stuffier by the second.

I wish I could say I handled the situation with grace and charm. I'd love to share how my dignified motherly responses served only to draw us closer to each other in love and harmony. They didn't. I grumped at Sami. I forgot her kind act from the morning and focused only on the mess. I knew she probably needed me to scoop her up and give her some love, but I didn't feel like I had it in me. In fact, I really just wanted to curl up under the covers and hide from the world for a week or two.

If only that were possible.

Unfortunately, as I look back on those preschool years with Sami, there were too many moments of grumpy misunderstandings and not enough gracious connections. There were times I was so overwhelmed that it spilled out on Sami and I wondered how I would make it another day, another week, another year on my own—or worse, how she would make it.

One of the hardest parts about those stressful times when money was short, when I was sick, or when something happened at work is that I added to my discouragement (and grumpy attitude) by being hard on myself. I heaped condemnation on top of whatever failing tackled my day, and that kept me discouraged even longer.

Maybe you understand. It could be that you've had a tough road as a single mom, and you wonder how you're going to make it through. Maybe finances are a big concern, or you're afraid of what the future will hold, or you're dealing with a frustrating situation with your ex-spouse. Maybe most days you feel pretty good, but then, like me, you hit a Saturday morning and find yourself overwhelmed and exhausted.

There are steps you can take in the midst of those moments—things you can do to take the edge off and face the world again. It's all about grace. Grace for you, grace for your little ones. So let's talk about what it means to live out that grace.

What You Can Do

In the past several chapters, I've talked about the kids' needs first, then your needs. But on this topic, I want to talk to you first. Because this is one of those big issues I don't want you to miss. You are an amazing woman. You're doing this alone. You're going to get frustrated, and you'll be tired; there'll be days you get it all right and days when you wonder who is inhabiting your body and who stole your smile. It's okay; it's part of the journey. So when you do feel overwhelmed and you've beaten yourself to the mat, remember these things.

Call out; let God comfort you. I can't tell you how many times I've gone to God embarrassed. I could almost envision myself walking toward him, my head hanging as I looked back on a day full of poor choices and lousy responses. It used to be that God was the last place I wanted to go when I messed everything up. Why would I want to go to a perfect God with all my mistakes? So I hid instead, usually in something that made me feel worse.

But thankfully, I've learned. I've learned that God is the safest place to go. I've learned about his character and how he loves it when we open our hearts to him—how he's ready and willing to help us when we've made a lousy choice. It's like our kids: if they make a mistake and try to hide it, it usually doesn't work. But if they make a mistake and run to us, and they're sorry, we can hold them close and give them what they need to make better choices in the future. We would never turn away our own child; why do we think God will turn us away?

We can go to God and he will remind us that even though there are moments when we are not enough, he is always enough. That he loves our children even more than we do, and he'll make up the difference in their lives. And somehow, after we pour out everything to him, we feel better—better able to handle the day, better able to love our kids, better able to do life well. The first place we should go when we're feeling overwhelmed is to the One who can help. He doesn't expect us to be perfect; he isn't surprised that we don't handle everything just right. He designed parenting to be a team effort, and since we don't have a husband right there to help, our God is more than ready and willing to step in and be that partner. When we go to him, we get all the grace we need to continue on.

Don't say anything to yourself that you wouldn't say to a friend. I can be so mean. It's true. I say things to myself that would make you cringe. I call myself names, I'm impatient, and I'm quick to criticize. Then I had a friend say something to me that has stuck with me. She said, "Elsa, don't say anything to yourself that you wouldn't say to a good friend." It stopped me in my tracks. I would never say to anyone else the things I say to myself. To everyone else, I extend grace; I comfort and say things like, "Well, of course you're grumpy, look at all the things you have going on—you have every right to be frustrated." But to myself, I say, "Come on, Elsa, you're being an idiot. Get over it. This is not a big deal." Think about it. Listen to your self-talk. And don't say anything to yourself that you wouldn't say to a dear friend.

Pamper yourself. Take a warm bath. Save up for a pedicure. Don't expect yourself to run full bore all the time. At some point, you need to take a deep breath, give yourself some grace, and be kind. Go out for ice cream, take a walk, call a friend to share a cup of tea. As you take care of yourself, you'll be better able to take care of the day.

Think of things you've done well. I'm very good at cataloguing my mistakes. I can tell you everything I've done wrong during the last twelve years on my own—probably in alphabetical order. But ask me what I've done right and I'll hang my head and have a hard time saying anything. It feels prideful or arrogant or somehow just wrong to celebrate those things. But honestly, my friend, we've done some things right on this journey. And sometimes we need to remember those things so we can continue making good choices.

See, I know you've sacrificed, you've worked hard, you're even reading this book in your desire to be a better mom. You have much to feel good about. Yes, you can look at all the things you've done wrong, all the moments when you were impatient or short with your children—but also take a moment and think of the things you've done right—the nights you stayed up when they were sick, the stories you've read, the extra hours you've worked to have money for Christmas or a birthday. If I could, I would wrap my arms around you and remind you of those things. "Well done," I would say. "Well done, my friend. Our God is so proud of you."

Take a break. Extend grace through time. Maybe you just need a little time on your own. Schedule that in. Call a friend and ask if they would be willing to watch your children for a Saturday afternoon so that you can go to Starbucks and read a book. It's nearly impossible to be "on" all the time. In my situation, Sami's dad lives far away, so she doesn't see him on weekends. If I want a break, I need to schedule that in and be strategic. If that's your situation as well, do take the time to schedule a little getaway. Give yourself time to breathe and the grace to seize that time.

If you can, make it right. I'm going to make mistakes. I've already proven that. If possible, I need to make it right. If I've been overly irritable with Sami, I can apologize. I can let her know I do make mistakes, but I want to make it right when I have the chance. Hopefully, as we own up to our mistakes, our kids will learn to do the same.

Extending Grace to Your Little Ones

We aren't the only ones who need a kind smile on a rough day, a get-out-of-the-grumpies card, a bit of sunshine when we least deserve it. Our kids need grace too. Boatloads of it. Here are some tips that may help you offer grace when it's the last thing you feel like doing.

See what might be underneath. We were walking through Wal-Mart when we saw them. A father and a little girl, about Sami's age, holding hands. The girl was looking up at her dad when we overheard her say, "Daddy, I love you so much!" He leaned over and picked her up. "I love you too!"

Just moments later, I told Sami she couldn't get the toy she wanted. She fell apart. Big tears rolled down her cheeks.

It was one of the few times when I really made the connection. She wasn't crying about the toy she couldn't have. She was crying about the daddy she couldn't have. She'd been watching the girl and her dad, her eyes focused on their every movement. I'd noticed. And in that moment, I could offer her the comfort she needed instead of getting angry about her tears.

Sometimes, just like us, our kids aren't responding to the immediate circumstance. They're responding to something else that hurts but is hard to define. Try to be aware of those moments.

Remember what matters. Amber was undone by a shoelace. Her little one, Andrew (a recently accomplished shoe-tier), was having a lousy day. He knew how to tie his shoe, but on this occasion, he was struggling. He looped the lace a few too many times, then sent the end through the wrong spot; every time he pulled it tight, it undid completely. Amber tried to point out his mistakes. He would have none of it. She tried to help. Absolutely not. "I can do it myself!" he insisted.

But they needed to be somewhere in twenty minutes, and Amber hated being late.

She told me the story with a rueful grin. "We didn't really have to be on time, but I wanted to be. It wasn't a big deal for him to work on his shoes for a few more minutes; we had the time to spare. He was figuring things out, doing it on his own, which was more important." Amber paused. "But I didn't see that then. Instead, I was angry. I was frustrated he wouldn't let me help. Finally, I raised my voice, took his shoes off, and made him put on his Velcro ones. Unfortunately, he's just sensitive enough that now he won't even try to tie his shoes anymore. We're starting from scratch."

Sometimes kids need us to see beyond the moment to what matters. Whether it's giving them a little extra time, offering patience, or remembering what's important, they need our grace and understanding in those moments.

Bottom line: If you are struggling in this area and find yourself with a short fuse, it might be helpful to take a break. Schedule in some down time by exchanging babysitting with another single parent, getting up early, or taking a walk. If your short fuse is a chronic problem, consider getting some counseling. It never hurts to get help on this road—there are people with good tools for handling this stuff. Don't be afraid to go to them. And remember, extending grace is easier when you're experiencing it yourself. Go back to those first suggestions and make them happen in your world. Cry out to God, watch the way you talk to yourself, and go for a little pampering. It helps.

Additional Resources

Heald, Cynthia. *Becoming a Woman of Grace*.

Lucado, Max. *Grace for the Moment, Inspirational Thoughts for Each Day of the Year*.

Rhea, Carolyn. *When Grief Is Your Constant Companion: God's Grace for a Woman's Heartache*.

Yancey, Philip. *What's So Amazing about Grace?*

19

Forgiveness

It was the third time in two weeks that Karen's daughter had been stood up by her dad. Karen ached to see her little girl standing by the window. "Daddy will be here soon, right?" Marie asked. "He said so!"

Karen nodded and turned back to her dinner preparations. "Please show up," she prayed urgently. "Please let him show up."

"What'd you say, Mama?" Marie asked.

"Nothing, sweet girl; I was talking to God."

As the minutes ticked by, Karen tried to keep her demeanor calm, even as the anger and sadness coursed through her. She hated to see her daughter hurting. This was the third time—the third time in a matter of weeks Jason hadn't shown up. The first time it was work. The second time it was an unexpected emergency at his house. But Karen had a different idea. She was pretty sure Jason was dating—and his time was now being spent with someone new. Unfortunately, it looked like Marie was going to spend another evening crying on her mom's bed.

"Mommy?" Marie was at her side, looking up with sad eyes. "Did Daddy forget again?"

"I'm not sure, love; let me give him a call."

Karen picked up the phone, knowing even as she dialed the numbers that he wouldn't answer. He never did. "Hi, Jason," she said brightly into the phone, knowing little eyes were watching. "Marie and I were just waiting for you. I know you're probably working late," she winked at her girl, "but Marie is excited to see you whenever you get home. Call us!"

With that, Karen set down the phone and scooped her girl up into her arms. "I'm sorry, honey," she said. "I know you're disappointed, but Daddy's probably just working. I'm sure he'll call soon."

But Daddy didn't call. He'd forgotten again. And Marie was heartbroken.

Karen shared her story with me, tears in her eyes. "You know what? I can handle when he hurts me. I don't like it, but I can work through it. What kills me is when Marie is hurt," Karen said. "He doesn't realize how much he means to her, and every time he blows her off, she thinks it's her fault. When I see her sadness, I could wring his neck. I know I'm supposed to forgive, but I don't know how to do that when it comes to her, and I sure don't know how to teach her to forgive him. I mean, she has every right to be angry and hurt. I'm not going to tell her it's okay and she needs to forgive him. There's no way."

A Forgiving Heart

I've felt like Karen. Maybe you have too. It could be your child's father is actively engaged and is a kind influence in his or her life. If that's the case, say a little prayer of thanksgiving and move on to the next chapter. But for many of us, when the father lets our child (or children) down, we somehow have to find a way to deal with our kids' anger and help them forgive. It doesn't come naturally, especially when we're having a tough time letting it go ourselves.

So here are some tips that may help you walk your child through his or her anger—toward forgiveness (we'll talk about how *you* can forgive a little later in the chapter).

Don't excuse your ex-spouse. A lot of times, to protect our child's heart, we'll excuse the ex. While this may be valid if they are rarely late, rarely grumpy, or only occasionally forgetful—it doesn't work when an ex consistently lets our child down. To excuse that behavior makes it seem okay for others to treat our children in a similar fashion. They won't learn healthy boundaries, and later on in life, when a boyfriend or husband dishonors them by their behavior or broken promises, we'll have trained our children to excuse it and allow the behavior to continue. Don't make excuses if there is a consistent problem in how your ex relates to your child.

Don't accuse your ex. Laying into how he is a "no-good, rotten, lousy father" isn't going to do much good either. Our children see themselves as half of the other parent. They identify with that parent so when we accuse or demean him, we are accusing and demeaning our own child. Avoid harsh words your child will internalize.

Acknowledge the hurt. When I'm hurting, people can offer advice, tell me not to hurt, get mad at the offending party, or offer any number of responses. But when someone puts her hand on my shoulder, looks me in the eyes, and says, "I'm sorry you're hurting," I almost always fall apart. The kindness in her eyes, the gentleness in her touch—I'm like putty in her hands. Often that is just what our children need. They need to know that it's okay to feel sad, that their anger is understandable, and that their feelings are valid. Sometimes simply holding them and allowing them to express their feelings is the very best response you can offer.

Affirm your child. Remind your child that Daddy's breaking a promise has nothing to do with who he or she is. Affirm and confirm his or her goodness, uniqueness, and how much you enjoy the time you spend together. You don't have to say anything demeaning about the ex to affirm how much you love and value your child.

Talk to your ex. If you have the type of relationship where you can be civil with each other, talk to your ex-spouse. Sometimes the broken promises have nothing to do with his forgetfulness and everything to do with his lack of understanding of how important he is to your child. Sometimes there's no maliciousness behind the behavior at all; he just doesn't see how much his love matters. So let him know, in a nonthreatening way, that his involvement, his love, and his encouragement will make a difference in your child's life.

What if none of that works? What happens if your child is hurt over and over? Then comfort your child over and over again. Affirm and encourage him or her and be the steady love, the steady influence in their world. They may be let down by one parent, but they can still know your consistent love and presence and comfort. And it will be your comfort, minus the excuses or the accusations, that will give them the freedom to feel their feelings and ultimately be able to forgive. But it takes time. They may hold on to their anger and frustration, which may even increase through their adolescent years. It won't work to say, "Forgive your father. God says to forgive, so forgive." Your child has every right to be angry and will probably have to feel that for a while.

What you can do is model forgiveness. Forgive those who offend you; as your child sees that forgiveness and freedom lived out in your world, she will be much more likely to forgive as well. But if you are holding on to stuff, clinging to bitterness, or constantly angry, it will be tough for your child to move through her anger in light of that.

Your Turn

So your child will be better able to forgive as you learn to forgive. Great. Sounds easy, right? Is it just a matter of speaking the words, waving some type of wand, and "moving on"?

If only. Unfortunately, some people do think that's all it takes. I had a woman once look at me in utter frustration. I was young and I was angry. "Elsa," she said, "you have to let this go. Just say the words. Say you forgive him and it'll be all done."

"Even if I don't mean it?"

"Yes, just say them and peace will flow through you."

"Really?"

"Really."

I said the words. It didn't work. No peace, no heavenly music wafting through the air, nothing. In fact, the next time I saw the man I was angry with, I wanted to wring his scrawny little neck. Nope, I wasn't exactly exuding forgiveness.

And when it comes to Sami, I have an even tougher time. When she is hurt by someone, the mama lioness in me comes out as I envision various torture devices that I could easily apply with just a little practice.

Maybe you can relate.

So what do we do? Let's look at some realistic steps to take as we approach forgiveness.

We need to understand forgiveness. Forgiveness doesn't mean that we are a doormat—that everything is okay and we feel warm fuzzies toward the person who offended us (you've hurt me and my child, and I'm okay with that). No. Forgiveness is choosing to release someone from the debt they owe you. And it's a choice that usually isn't accompanied by sweet feelings. It's understanding that by holding on to our bitterness and resentment, we'll be the ones held captive. It's realizing we've hurt others, maybe not quite as badly, but we've made our fair share of poor choices. And that we're all broken people in need of forgiveness. Forgiveness is knowing that if we do hold on to the anger that's come to define us, there won't be much joy for the future.

Feel the emotion. We must take the first step. Just as it is with our kids, we need to feel the emotion that comes from being wronged. We need to be angry, to feel the hurt, to cry if we must. If our child has been hurt (or continues to experience hurt feelings), we can't just sweep our reaction under the rug. We need to get the emotion out—whether that's with a safe friend (who knows your heart and will let you vent without telling you what you should feel), through a journal, or in a letter. I've written many letters I've never sent. I don't edit myself or stop midway to check sentence structure; I just go for it. I write out every feeling, no matter how immature. I vent, I yell, I get the bitterness down on paper. Without feeling the emotion, it's impossible to move past it to authentic forgiveness. We need to process those things first—before we can move forward.

Remember, God is just. Sometimes the reason we don't want to let go of our anger is we're afraid this person who offended us or our child will get away scot-free. Wiping the slate clean seems unfair because that will make it seem as if their behavior was okay. Well, don't forget, there are always consequences to our choices; God designed that for each of our lives. If your ex is breaking promises to your child, that behavior will have a consequence on their relationship. Sure, forgiveness may be extended, but that relationship is still damaged, and he will have to deal with that. That same behavior will have consequences on his other relationships as well—no one who chooses to demean others gets away unscathed.

As far as your child, your own heart, and the damage done—God also does amazing work with broken hearts. As we seek him out and learn about the love he has for us, he has a way of binding up broken pieces and then, beyond expectation, turning them into strength. It may sound simplistic, but it's truth. Nothing that has happened to you or your child has escaped God's notice. He will fight on your behalf, and if you choose to seek him, he will definitely use those broken pieces to fashion a masterpiece. It's what he does. This very truth is what makes it safe to forgive—God's nature and his character. Once you know that about him, it's much easier to let go of your anger.

Forgiveness takes time. My mom was in a concentration camp for four years as a child. She witnessed atrocities no one should ever have to see. As she grew to adulthood she suffered from post-traumatic stress disorder. The war, and the depression from the war, robbed her of so much life. My mom had many people to forgive—the Japanese soldiers who had tortured her family, her parents for not being there for her. . . .

When I ask my mom about her story now, she's able to say that she has forgiven them all. But it did not happen with simple words and a wave of a magical spiritual wand. It was a daily choice. "First I had to deal with the emotions—the anger, the betrayal, the sadness. I did that with counselors and friends. Then, when it came to forgiving them, I first had to do it a hundred times a day. Every time the thought came up, and it came up a lot, I said, 'I've forgiven this,' and try to think of something else."

Months later, the thought would come up twenty times a day, then ten, then once. Finally, it diminished to once a week, once a year. "Now," Mom says, "it doesn't come up at all. I don't hold anything against the people who harmed my family and me. But it took time. It took a long time."

Bottom line: Forgiveness is a process, not a warm fuzzy. You need to experience the feelings and then work through to the forgiveness, and you truly need to know that God has your back—and your child's. And as you move through the process, you will find the freedom you've been longing for.

If you're in a situation where you consistently have to forgive (for example, the story at the beginning of the chapter, where broken promises may need to be forgiven over and over again), stay on top of it. Don't let bitterness define you and don't let that happen in your child. It is hard work, but deal with those emotions and keep yourself free from the trap of hatred and bitterness. Trust in the One who can use all of that stuff to bring about strength, compassion, and faith. That's more than a spiritual nicety applied to harsh reality. It's truth. When we know that God is bigger, we can enjoy and experience peace. He does make it right.

Additional Resources

God Wants Me to Forgive Them?!? Classic Veggie Tales DVD.
Kendall, R. T. *Total Forgiveness.*
MacArthur, John. *The Freedom and Power of Forgiveness.*
Mullins, Traci. *Embracing Forgiveness* (Women of Faith Series).
Scripture Teacher's Books: Solomon and Friends Learn about Forgiveness.
Stanley, Charles. *The Gift of Forgiveness.*

20

God

I used to think God was far away. He certainly wasn't involved in my world. He was distant—and angry. I figured he was also disappointed, especially when it came to me. I had made so many lousy choices I didn't think he would ever want anything to do with me. I could see where he would forgive others (and often told them so), but when it came to me, I couldn't seem to grasp it. Why? Because I should have known better. I should have made different choices. I should have been a better daughter, sister, friend, wife . . . human being. I should, I should.

So when people told me of a loving God who was profoundly interested in my world, I may have nodded politely, but inside I scoffed at the idea. Why would he want anything to do with me? I wasn't stupid; I knew where I'd been. I started off my single motherhood a mess. I was ashamed of who I was so I longed for someone to tell me I was worth something, anything—which of course, brought me to choices that made things messier. I longed for affection. I was addicted to cigarettes. My finances were in shambles. I was in survival mode, so I did what I needed to do to take care of myself. If that included lying, I lied. If that included hurting someone else, I did so. Never without regret, but I still did it—thinking the life I'd fallen into was all the life I would ever know. I had to grab whatever little moments of joy I could. At whatever the cost.

Things are different now. These last twelve years as a single parent have changed everything. It started as I encountered people—people who loved me in spite of my mess. They looked at me with eyes of compassion and extended a helping hand. Oh, not everyone. There were definitely those who were quick to judge, but there were others—others who lived and talked about a God I could see in their eyes. Theirs was a God who didn't base his love on performance but who loved because he *is* love and it wouldn't even cross his mind to deny me his grace.

I wanted their God, because the one I had crafted in my mind—the one with the arms folded, the foot tapping, and the disapproving grimace—didn't line up with what they were teaching me and living before me. So I watched these Jesus lovers, and when I let them into my world I discovered they weren't so different from me. Many of them had stories similar to my own. And they didn't talk about God as a distant being; they talked about him as a reality in their world, as a friend and confidant, as a loving Father.

Slowly I began to get to know God for myself. I went to the Bible and I went to him in prayer. I told him what

I thought. I told him how I wanted to know him for who he really was. And I told him that I wanted to love him, if only he would show me how.

He did. Oh how he did! I love our God so much. Unashamedly, with all my heart, with all my being. He is good and faithful. He is kind and gracious. He is strong and holy. He is a Father to the fatherless, and I have seen him work in our lives. Miracles have abounded over the last twelve years. He showed up everywhere—sometimes in a way that would cause me to tremble, sometimes in ways that made me laugh out loud. And it's not as if once I said yes to him, I became some kind of super-spiritual single mom. Yes, I've grown, but I've also stumbled. I've fallen off the path and into the bushes; I've wandered off the trail thinking something in the woods looked more fun. Sometimes I chose him and sometimes I chose myself. But he hasn't abandoned me (and he never will). And he never has, and never will, abandon you.

When I think back on the last twelve years, I've seen God's hand in so many ways: he's supplied finances, friendship, and accountability. He's allowed me to hurt but then dried up my tears. He's used the bad and ushered in the good. He's taken every broken piece, every one, and crafted them into something useful and beautiful. He's comforted my broken heart; he's ushered in unexpected and delightful surprises. He is good and he is able. Honestly, he is everything that we need on this journey. He is all that you need, all that your children need. While the tips in this book may be helpful to the practical world of single momhood, the best tip I can ever offer you is this: get to know our God.

What You Can Do

My friends, I finish off that last paragraph with tears in my eyes. I can imagine you reading it, and I wonder how you feel. Are my words encouraging? Or do they make you angry? Maybe you and God haven't been on such good terms lately. You may wonder if he hears your cries or sees your world. Maybe you feel abandoned and don't want anything to do with religion and all that comes with it. Or maybe the last paragraph stirred something in you, a longing to know this God at a deeper level. Know this: wherever you are on the spectrum of emotion, you are loved. Not in the cheesy "Jesus loves you" bumper-sticker kind of way. But in the amazing, profound, life-changing way that catches your tears in a bottle, that hears every heart-wrenching sigh, that longs to be a part of your world with a depth you will never truly understand. So please, read through the rest of this chapter, and if you do nothing else in this book, get to know our God better. Use some of these tools to reach out to him. It will be worth every bit of effort you extend. He is ready and willing and able to meet you.

Get around his people. You'll recognize the place that has God's fingerprints all over it. When I first showed up at the women's ministry at my brother's church, I met all kinds of amazing women. At first, I thought they were pretty good fakers. They had the smile, the right clothes, and the good hair. But as I got to know them, I realized they weren't faking at all; I was just being critical. They were, in fact, genuine and authentic. And I wanted to know more. Being around warm and contagious people will open our eyes to the reality of God. Whether it's your MOPS group or a singles ministry or a women's ministry, try some different places. Risk. Step out of your shell. Share a little of your story. If you aren't received, move on. But if you are, if you see the smiles and hear the affirmation and see the acceptance, risk a little more. Don't give up. If you run into a wall, try a different group. You'll know the one that oozes the kindness of our God. The members won't be able to hide it—it'll spill out of their eyes and through their hugs. When you find that place, settle in. Risk. Commit. Learn. It will change everything.

Read his love letter. I used to dread reading the Bible. I'd open it up, read something that had nothing to do with my life and world (or so I thought), and wonder how people got so excited about what I considered an ancient book written by ancient men. But then I ran into Jennifer. What a beautiful lover of God's Word! She would get so excited about something she read; with eyes shining she'd say, "You know what our God says, Elsa? He says . . ." and she'd open up to a particular passage and read. Suddenly, I'd discover what she read had direct application in my life. So with her help, I began to dig around a little more. And it was there; right there in Scripture I found out about the depth of compassion God has for us, how Jesus reaches out to broken women, how my past didn't have to define me, and how God had a hope and a future in mind for me. I was amazed as I discovered that this ancient book was actually a modern-day love letter written to address my real-life issues. What a delight to find all that wisdom at my fingertips!

Talk to him. I know we devoted a whole chapter to this, but I just wanted to reiterate—be real with God! If you are growing in your relationship, let him know your heart and passion to know him better. If you don't love him but want to learn how, lay that out there as well. If you're angry or hurting, don't be afraid to call out to him in real ways. God hears your prayers; he bends his ear to you. You are his beloved. No matter what you're feeling, let him know, and then look, listen, and be aware of how he may respond.

Worship him. I used to look at worship in one way— people standing in church, some bored, some engaged, but everyone singing. I figured that if I didn't connect with God during worship in church, there was probably something wrong with me . . . or my relationship with God. The truth is, I'm wired differently. I feel most connected to God when I walk outside. There is something about his creativity in nature that always seems to capture my heart. Or rather than singing in church, I find I love singing in the quiet of my living room. At church I get distracted by all the other people around me or by the band or a fly buzzing around, anything. The last thing I think about in church worship is the One I am supposed to be worshiping! So I've learned. According to my wiring, it works best to sing in the quiet of my home or worship him as I walk outdoors. Not that I've stopped going to church (that is still my community), but I've learned not to beat myself up if I don't hear the angels singing during the praise set.

How do you like to worship God? Maybe you like to write, and writing out poetry or prayers is an act of worship. Maybe you enjoy the outdoors too, or music or art. You are wired to express your heart for God in a very unique way—explore different options and see what most connects your heart to his. What you will discover in the process is that God will meet you however you come to him—and while you may begin worshiping with the idea to bless him, you will find that you will always walk away feeling his delight in return. It's just his way!

Seek out a mentor. There's someone who has walked where you are walking. There's someone who knows how you're feeling and can offer some insight into those chaotic moments of single parenthood. Find that person! I used to think God would drop a mentor from the sky for me. She would see me at church or at a small group; she'd seek me out and desire to pour all of her wisdom into my unsightly world. It didn't happen that way.

I have had mentors, but only because I sought them out. I looked for women who were authentically in love with Christ; I bribed them with donuts, coffee, or a lunch at my home; and I listened. I absorbed. Like a sponge. I wanted what they had, so I put myself around them. And if they didn't have the time (and bubbly, authentic believers usually don't; they have full lives of investing already), I'd wait until they were alone in a hallway and stalk them for wise counsel (okay, not really). But if you want someone to pour into you, look around, be determined, and keep asking (not the same person obviously, but keep looking and asking). A mentor will help you draw closer to our God.

Be a mentor. Someone needs you. Someone needs to know the things you've learned. Someone is where you have been—and she needs to know she's not alone. It's amazing how you will get to know God as you live out being his hands and feet. Some single parents simply view themselves as the victim. They think they don't have anything to offer anyone because of what they've been through. But think about it: you have so much to offer. You're doing this alone! You're a survivor! You're stronger than you know and more resilient than you thought. You've learned to take care of your child, your finances, your home. And maybe not everything is running smoothly, but you have discovered in yourself a strength you didn't know existed. And someone else needs it.

Reach out to someone ahead of you. Reach out to someone behind you. And watch how much closer you will draw to God as you do both. He will work in your life and through your life, and there's something about this reality that will draw you to the very heart of him. You're needed. Someone will learn best from what you have to teach. In other words, there are people out there who won't learn from me, from the pastor, from anyone else. They're wired to best hear about God from you and your life circumstances. When you participate in what God is doing in someone's story, life takes on an entirely new meaning—and everything you've gone through, every tear you've cried, suddenly has the most beautiful and tremendous value. Reach out.

Bottom line: As you get to know God by putting yourself in community, praying, reading his love letter, worshiping, mentoring, and being mentored, life will take on a sweetness you've never known. Your child will benefit as he or she sees you loving God and loving others. Think about this: I've told you some of my story—my messiness, selfishness, and disobedience. Well, just a few weeks ago, my daughter and I were sitting at the kitchen table looking over some evaluations of a talk I had given at a conference. She was reading through the comments, and tears came to her eyes. "Listen to this one, Mom," she said. "It says, 'Elsa shines with the light of Christ; it pours out of her. I want to be just like her.'" Sami put down the piece of paper and hugged me close. "I'm so proud of you, Mom." She pulled back and put her hand on my face. "I want to be like you too."

I couldn't stop the tears. Because I know where I've been. And all that is good in me came as I really began to know and love God. He changed everything. And if Sami wants to be like me, it's only because Jesus did something in my heart that I could never do without him. He changed me. Friend, aside from every tip presented in this book, if you want to parent your preschooler well, if you want to be a light in his or her life, seek our God first. He will shine through you in a way that will point your precious one to the only source of real hope.

Additional Resources

Bunch, Cindy. *Woman of God*.

Healing the Heart, Focus on the Family Women's Series Bible Study.

Kok, Elsa. *A Woman Who Hurts, A God Who Heals*.

LePeau, Phyllis J. *Women of the New Testament*.

Moore, Beth. *Breaking Free*.

About MOPS

You take care of your children, Mom. Who takes care of you? MOPS® International (Mothers of Preschoolers) provides mothers of preschoolers with the nurture and resources they need to be the best moms they can be.

MOPS is dedicated to the message that "mothering matters" and that moms of young children need encouragement during these critical and formative years. Chartered groups meet in approximately 4,500 churches and Christian ministries throughout the United States and in thirty-five other countries. Each MOPS program helps mothers find friendship and acceptance, provides opportunities for women to develop and practice leadership skills in the group, and promotes spiritual growth. MOPS groups are chartered ministries of local churches and meet at a variety of times and locations: daytime, evenings, and on weekends; in churches, homes, and workplaces.

The MOPPETS program offers a loving, learning experience for children while their moms attend MOPS.

Other MOPS resources include *MOMSense*®magazine and radio, the MOPS International website, and books and resources available through the MOPShop.

There are 14.3 million mothers of preschoolers in the United States alone, and many moms can't attend a local MOPS group. These moms still need the support that MOPS International can offer! For a small registration fee, any mother of preschoolers can join the MOPS to Mom Connection® and receive *MOMSense* magazine six times a year, a weekly Mom-E-Mail message of encouragement, and other valuable benefits.

Find out how MOPS International can help you become part of the MOPS to Mom Connection and/or join or start a MOPS group. Visit our website at www. MOPS.org. Phone us at 303-733-5353. Or email Info@ MOPS.org. To learn how to start a MOPS group, call 1-888-910-MOPS.

Elsa Kok Colopy is the former Single-Parent Family editor for the *Focus on the Family* magazine. She is the author of three other books: *A Woman Who Hurts, A God Who Heals*; *A Woman with a Past, a God with a Future*; and *Settling for Less Than God's Best? A Relationship Checkup for Single Women.* A mom with twelve years of single-parenting experience, Elsa works as a freelance writer and speaker and lives with her husband and children in Bella Vista, Arkansas.